SHE LEADS WITH AI

HOW HIGH-ACHIEVING WOMEN USE AI TO RECLAIM TIME, REDUCE BURNOUT, AND LEAD WITH CONFIDENCE

T. RENEE' SMITH

She Leads With AI: How High-Achieving Women Use AI to Reclaim Time, Reduce Burnout, and Lead with Confidence

Copyright © 2025 T. Reneé Smith

All rights reserved. No part of this book may be reproduced, stored in a retrieval system, or transmitted in any form or by any means—electronic, mechanical, photocopy, recording, or otherwise—without prior written permission of the publisher, except for brief quotations in critical reviews or articles.

ISBN: 978-1-7331858-9-9
Printed in the United States of America

IMPORTANT DISCLAIMERS

AI Technology Disclaimer: The AI landscape evolves at unprecedented speed. Tools, features, and capabilities mentioned in this book reflect the state of AI at the time of writing. By the time you read this, new innovations will have emerged, and some tools may have changed or evolved. The strategies and frameworks provided are designed to remain relevant regardless of specific tools. Always conduct your own research and due diligence when selecting AI tools for your personal or professional use.

Results Disclaimer: The strategies and examples shared in this book represent the experiences of individual women and organizations. Your results will vary based on your unique circumstances, commitment to implementation, and chosen tools. Success requires consistent action, not just information.

Medical and Legal Disclaimer: This book provides general information and should not replace professional medical, legal, financial, or psychological advice. Always consult qualified professionals for decisions affecting your health, legal matters, finances, or mental wellbeing.

Privacy and Security Notice: When using AI tools, always review privacy policies and terms of service. Be mindful of what personal or proprietary information you share with AI systems. Protect sensitive data and maintain appropriate security measures.

Faith and Spirituality: While this book includes faith-based perspectives and spiritual insights, it respects all belief systems. Take what serves you and leave what doesn't.

Community Invitation: For ongoing support, updated tool recommendations, and connection with like-minded women, visit treneesmith.com.

DEDICATION

To my husband, the secret genius behind this book.

You introduced me to AI when I was skeptical, showed me tools when I was overwhelmed, and painted a vision of the future when I could barely see past my AI fatigue. When I wanted to quit (multiple times), you reminded me why this mattered. Your wisdom, insight, and unwavering belief in what AI could mean for women like me made this book possible.

You're not just my partner in life; you're the visionary who helped me see what others couldn't yet imagine. This book exists because you refused to let me give up on AI, or myself.

To my precious children, thank you for sharing your mama with the world.

Your patience as I navigate being a wife, mom, CEO, daughter, friend, author, and all the other roles I play has not gone unnoticed. Every time you understood when I needed to work, every hug when I was stressed, every "You got this, Mom," you were part of creating this book. You inspire me to build a future where technology serves love, not replaces it.

DEDICATION

To every woman standing at the crossroads, this is for you.

The one trying to prepare for constant AI changes while keeping your human touch intact. The one who wants to embrace the future without losing your soul. The one who knows there must be a way to have both technological power and human wisdom. You're not behind. You're not too late. You're exactly where you need to be.

And to God, thank You for the nudges that became pushes.

The whispers that became clear direction, and the spiritual downloads that filled these pages. Every time I sat down to write, I felt You guiding my thoughts and moving my fingers across the keyboard. This book is as much Yours as it is mine. May it serve Your purpose of helping Your daughters rise into all You've created them to be.

> "With God, all things are possible - even learning AI."
>
> —T. RENEE' SMITH

TABLE OF CONTENTS

PREFACE: A NOTE FROM T. RENEÉ 1

INTRODUCTION 7
    TRUTH BOMB- I DIDN'T WRITE THIS BOOK BECAUSE I LOVE TECH 7
    MY MAMA BEAR MOMENT WITH AI 8
    WHY I'M YOUR GUIDE THROUGH THIS AI REVOLUTION 9
    WHAT THIS BOOK REALLY IS (AND WHAT IT DEFINITELY ISN'T) 11
    THE WOMEN YOU'LL MEET 12
    YOUR JOURNEY THROUGH THIS BOOK 13
    WHAT YOU'RE REALLY GOING TO GET 13
    THE MOVEMENT WE'RE BUILDING 14
    A PERSONAL PROMISE 15

PART I: THE MINDSET SHIFT 17

    THE FIVE SHIFTS THAT ACTUALLY MATTER 18
    THE TRUTH ABOUT YOUR RESISTANCE 19
    WHAT THIS IS REALLY ABOUT 20
    WHY THESE MINDSET SHIFTS MATTER RIGHT NOW 20
    HOW TO USE THIS SECTION 21
    WHERE THIS JOURNEY LEADS 21

CHAPTER 1: FROM CHAOS TO CLARITY: YOUR AI AWAKENING 23
    THE AI TRAINING THAT SHOOK MY CONFIDENCE 23
        What if I was asking the wrong question entirely? 24
    THE REAL REASON YOU'RE SCARED (AND WHY THAT'S ACTUALLY
    GOOD NEWS) 24

How This Really Looks in Practice...25
The Work-Life Integration Truth...27
Sarah's Discovery: When AI Became Her Lifeline.....................................27
What AI Is (And Why That Should Relieve You)..28
The Elevation Principle 30
Your Work in the AI Age...31
Take a Pause, Friend 33
Do This Now, Not Later..33
A Personal Note 34
Chapter 1 Quick Reference 35

CHAPTER 2: THE PERMISSION YOU'VE BEEN WAITING FOR 37
The Text That Hit Too Close to Home..37
The Myth of the Woman Who Needs Nothing 38
Jennifer's Breaking Point Became Her Breakthrough 39
The Hidden Cost of Doing It All 41
The Permission Slip You've Been Waiting For 42
What Accepting Support Actually Looks Like...43
The Resistance Is Real (And That's Okay)...43
Take a Pause, Friend 45
Do This Now, Not Later..45
A Personal Note 47
Chapter 2 Quick Reference 48

CHAPTER 3: FROM EITHER/OR TO EVERYTHING 49
When My Husband Called Me Out...49
Maria's AND Life Revolution 52
The New Success Metrics 53
The Fear That Keeps Us Stuck 53
Take a Pause, Friend 55
Do This Now, Not Later..55
A Personal Note 57
Chapter 3 Quick Reference 58

CHAPTER 4: WHY WOMEN ARE THE FUTURE OF AI LEADERSHIP 59
The Tech Conference That Made Me Laugh (And Then Get Mad).......59
What's Really Happening in AI Leadership Right Now...........................60
Sarah's Story: When Heart Meets Hard Data...63
Why AI Desperately Needs Women's Leadership 63

TABLE OF CONTENTS

THE POWER OF INVOLVING WOMEN IN THE AI CONVERSATION 64
WHAT CHANGES WHEN WOMEN LEAD AI 65
   But What If I'm Not Technical? 65
TAKE A PAUSE, FRIEND 67
DO THIS NOW, NOT LATER 68
A PERSONAL NOTE 70
CHAPTER 4 QUICK REFERENCE 71

CHAPTER 5: BUILDING YOUR AI CONFIDENCE 73
MY 100 FAILURES BEFORE MY FIRST WIN 73
THE CONFIDENCE MYTH THAT'S KEEPING YOU STUCK 74
MICHELLE'S JOURNEY: FROM I CAN'T TO I TEACH THIS NOW 75
THE REAL CONFIDENCE KILLERS (AND YOUR POWER MOVES) 76
YOUR CONFIDENCE-BUILDING ROADMAP 77
THE QUESTIONS THAT BUILD REAL CONFIDENCE 79
TAKE A PAUSE, FRIEND 80
DO THIS NOW, NOT LATER 80
WHAT HAPPENS WHEN YOU BUILD AI CONFIDENCE 81
A PERSONAL NOTE 82
CHAPTER 5 QUICK REFERENCE 83

PART II: AI FOR YOUR SOUL: SPIRITUALITY, SELF-CARE & INNER WORK 85

THE 'PICK A LANE' TRAP THAT'S STEALING OUR JOY 86
WHAT THIS SECTION WILL ACTUALLY DO FOR YOUR LIFE 87
THE INTEGRATION REVOLUTION (AND WHY IT'S ABOUT TIME) 88

CHAPTER 6: AI FOR YOUR SOUL: SPIRITUALITY, SELF-CARE & INNER WORK 91
THE PRAYER THAT STARTED EVERYTHING 91
THE BOTH/AND APPROACH TO TECHNOLOGY AND SPIRITUALITY 92
MEET CARMEN: FROM SPIRITUAL BURNOUT TO SACRED PARTNERSHIP 93
HOW I USE AI TO DEEPEN MY SPIRITUAL PRACTICE 95
TAKE A PAUSE, FRIEND 97
REAL SELF-CARE VS. INSTAGRAM SELF-CARE 98
DO THIS NOW, NOT LATER 99
CHAPTER 6 QUICK REFERENCE 100

CHAPTER 7: AI FOR YOUR BODY: HEALTH, FITNESS & WELLNESS THAT ACTUALLY WORKS ... 101

The Whole Foods Existential Crisis (Population: Me) ... 101
The Health Information Chaos That's Stealing Our Peace ... 102
Meet Diana: From Health Perfectionism to Sustainable Wellness ... 103
How I Use AI as My Personal Wellness Team ... 105
Take a Pause, Friend ... 107
The Real Reason Most Health Plans Fail Women Like Us ... 108
Do This Now, Not Later ... 109
Advanced AI Health Strategies ... 110
When to Seek Professional Medical Support ... 110
Chapter 7 Quick Reference ... 111

CHAPTER 8: AI FOR YOUR HEART: RELATIONSHIPS & EMOTIONAL INTELLIGENCE ... 113

The Fight That Taught Me About True Communication in Marriage ... 113
The Communication Crisis Nobody's Talking About ... 114
Meet Jasmine: From People-Pleasing to Authentic Connection ... 115
How I Use AI to Strengthen My Relationships ... 117
Take a Pause, Friend ... 118
The Real Reason Relationships Feel Harder Than They Used To ... 119
Do This Now, Not Later ... 121
Beyond the Basics: Advanced Relationship Strategies ... 122
Chapter 8 Quick Reference ... 123

CHAPTER 9: AI FOR YOUR MIND: MENTAL & EMOTIONAL HEALTH ... 125

The Day My Therapist Drew Me a Picture That Opened My Eyes ... 125
What Success Actually Costs Us Mentally ... 127
Meet Erica: From Beauty Industry Pressure to Inner Confidence ... 128
How I Use AI for Daily Mental Wellness ... 130
Take a Pause, Friend ... 132
The Superwoman Cape That's Choking Us ... 133
Do This Now, Not Later ... 134
When to Seek Professional Support ... 135
Chapter 9 Quick Reference ... 136

TABLE OF CONTENTS

CHAPTER 10: AI FOR YOUR ENVIRONMENT: HOME, SPACE & LIFE ORGANIZATION.. 137
- The Tuesday Evening Clean Up Before the Housekeeper Comes 137
- The Mind-Environment Connection 138
- Meet Maya: From Divorce Chaos to I've Got This Confidence 139
- How I Use AI to Create a Home That Actually Works 141
- Take a Pause, Friend 143
- Why Most Organization Advice Doesn't Work for Busy Women 144
- Do This Now, Not Later 146
- Chapter 10 Quick Reference 148

CHAPTER 11: YOUR AI DREAM TEAM: LIVING LIKE YOU HAVE A PERSONAL STAFF (WITHOUT THE CELEBRITY BUDGET) 149
- The Morning That Made Me Feel Like Oprah (But Better) 149
- The Celebrity Secret We Can All Access Now 151
- Meet Aria: Living Like a Multi-Industry Mogul 152
- How I Built My AI Support Team 154
- Take a Pause, Friend 156
- How Celebrities Really Get Things Done (And You Can Too) 157
- Building Your AI Dream Team 158
- Do This Now, Not Later 159
- Advanced Celebrity-Level Strategies 160
- Chapter 11 Quick Reference 162

PART III: THE MULTI-ROLE WOMAN: LEADING IN LOVE, FAMILY, BUSINESS & LIFE   163

- The Day I Realized I Was Playing Everyone But Myself..................... 163
- The Role-Playing Trap We All Fall Into 164
  - *What This Section Will Do for Your Life* 165
  - *The Integration, Not Balance, Approach* 166

CHAPTER 12: SHE LEADS AS A WIFE & PARTNER: DANCING BETWEEN BOSS AND BELOVED 169
- The Conversation Where I Almost Chose My Ego Over My Marriage 169
- The High-Achieving Woman's Energy Evolution 171
- Meet Victoria: When the Breadwinner Has to Learn to Be the Bride 172

    Meet Sofia: When Your Marriage Gets Your Leftovers 176
    How I Use AI for Marriage Energy Management 179
    Mastering Your Masculine-Feminine Flow 180
    Take a Pause, Friend 183
    Beyond Management: AI for Marriage Ministry 184
    Do This Now, Not Later 185
    Chapter 12 Quick Reference 187

CHAPTER 13: SHE LEADS AS A MOM: RAISING TINY HUMANS WHO THINK THEY RUN THE WORLD 189
    The Prayer That Backfired Spectacularly 189
    The Strong-Willed Child Reality Check 190
    Meet Amanda: Blending Families Without Losing Your Sanity 191
    Meet Linda: Single Parenting with Humor and Strategy 194
    How I Use AI for Real-World Motherhood 196
    The "Good Mom" Myth That's Completely Wrong 198
    Take a Pause, Friend 200
    Do This Now, Not Later 202
    Chapter 13 Quick Reference 203

CHAPTER 14: SHE LEADS AS A DAUGHTER & FAMILY MEMBER: THE TRUTH ABOUT BEING THE SUCCESSFUL ONE 205
    The Hospital Room That Made Me Chief Medical Officer (Without My Permission) 205
    The Success Tax Nobody Warns You About 207
    Meet Brooke: When Caregiving Becomes a Full-Time Job You Didn't Apply For 208
    Meet Patricia: When "You Work for Yourself" Means "You're Always Available" 211
    How I Use AI for Family Relationships That Actually Work 214
    The Hidden Cost of Being Everyone's Everything 216
    Take a Pause, Friend 218
    Beyond Rescue Mode: AI for Sustainable Family Support 219
    Do This Now, Not Later 220
    Chapter 14 Quick Reference 221

CHAPTER 15: SHE LEADS AS A FRIEND & COMMUNITY MEMBER 223
    The Day I Realized I Was Surrounded by People but Felt Alone 223
    The Surface-Level Friendship Trap 225

    THE INVESTMENT VS. AVAILABILITY MYTH 225
    MY JOURNEY FROM LONELY TO CONNECTED 226
    MY HEARTFELT PRAYER TO GOD 227
    TAKE A PAUSE, FRIEND 230
    AI AS YOUR FRIENDSHIP ENHANCEMENT PARTNER 230
    REAL-WORLD AI FRIENDSHIP APPLICATIONS 231
    DO THIS NOW, NOT LATER 232
    A COACH'S NOTE 232
    CHAPTER 15 QUICK REFERENCE 233

CHAPTER 16: SHE LEADS AS A PROFESSIONAL **235**
    THE BOARDROOM WHERE EVERYTHING CLICKED 235
    THE LEADERSHIP PARADOX THAT'S HOLDING YOU BACK 237
    MARIA'S 90-DAY LEADERSHIP BREAKTHROUGH 237
    TAKE A PAUSE, FRIEND 240
    PROFESSIONAL AI STRATEGIES FOR LEADERS 241
    ADVANCED PROFESSIONAL STRATEGIES FOR LEADERS 243
    REAL-WORLD IMPLEMENTATION EXAMPLES 245
    DO THIS NOW, NOT LATER 246
    A COACH'S NOTE 247
    CHAPTER 16 QUICK REFERENCE 248

CHAPTER 17: SHE LEADS AS A CEO & BUSINESS OWNER **251**
    THE THREE-YEAR DEAL THAT ALMOST STOLE MY SOUL 251
    THE CEO TRAP NOBODY WARNS YOU ABOUT 253
    WHY WOMEN ENTREPRENEURS NEED THIS MORE THAN ANYONE 254
    RACHEL'S PR STORY: WHEN AI THREATENED EVERYTHING SHE'D BUILT 255
    THE CLIENT REALITY CHECK 256
    RACHEL'S AI TRANSFORMATION: FROM BASIC TO BRILLIANT 257
    RACHEL'S PREDICTIVE PR STRATEGY 258
    THE ART OF PROMPT ENGINEERING 258
    STRATEGIC PR THAT ACTUALLY DRIVES REVENUE 259
    TAKE A PAUSE, FRIEND 261
    CEO AI STRATEGIES THAT ACTUALLY WORK 262
    ADVANCED CEO STRATEGIES (WHEN YOU'RE READY TO LEVEL UP) 266
    REAL-WORLD CEO TRANSFORMATIONS THAT INSPIRE 268
    DO THIS NOW, NOT LATER 269
    A COACH'S NOTE 270
    CHAPTER 17 QUICK REFERENCE 271

PART IV: YOUR AI-POWERED FUTURE   273

PART IV: YOUR AI-POWERED FUTURE 273
WHAT YOU'LL DISCOVER IN THIS SECTION: 274

CHAPTER 18: YOUR PERSONAL AI STRATEGIC ROADMAP: FROM OVERWHELM TO OWNERSHIP 277

WHEN RESEARCH ALMOST BROKE MY BRAIN (AND WHY THAT'S GOOD NEWS FOR YOU) 277
STRATEGY FIRST, TOOLS SECOND 279
T.I.M.E HUMAN-CENTERED AI™ STRATEGY FRAMEWORK: YOUR STRATEGIC FOUNDATION 280
YOUR THREE STRATEGIC SPHERES 281
Building Your Strategic Roadmap Using T.I.M.E Human-Centered AI™ Strategy Framework *281*
TAKE A PAUSE, FRIEND: QUICK REALITY CHECK 289
STRATEGIC DECISION FRAMEWORK 290
YOUR LIVING ROADMAP 291
STRATEGIC WISDOM FROM THE JOURNEY 291
DO THIS NOW, NOT LATER 292
A COACH'S NOTE 293
CHAPTER 18 QUICK REFERENCE 293

CHAPTER 19: LEADING YOUR ORGANIZATION'S AI TRANSFORMATION 295

THE CEO WHO ALMOST STARTED AN OFFICE UPRISING 295
WHY MOST AI INITIATIVES FAIL (AND HOW YOURS WON'T) 296
THE G.U.I.D.E. FRAMEWORK FOR HUMAN-CENTERED AI™ TRANSFORMATION: YOUR ORGANIZATIONAL AI STRATEGY 297
TAKE A PAUSE, LEADER: YOUR READINESS REALITY CHECK 300
REAL SUCCESS METRICS THAT MATTER 305
COMMON PITFALLS AND HOW TO AVOID THEM 306
YOUR 90-DAY QUICK START GUIDE 307
DO THIS NOW, NOT LATER 308
A COACH'S NOTE 309
CHAPTER 19 QUICK REFERENCE 310

CHAPTER 20: WRITING HISTORY-WOMEN WHO LEAD AI TRANSFORMATION 313

WHEN WOMEN SHOW UP, EVERYTHING CHANGES 313
WHY THIS MOMENT NEEDS US SPECIFICALLY 314

THE PLOT TWIST NOBODY SEES COMING 315
YOUR INVITATION TO HISTORY-MAKING 316
    How to Position Yourself as a History-Maker (Not a History-Watcher) ... 317
THE THREE WAVES OF WOMEN'S AI LEADERSHIP 318
WHAT HISTORY WILL SAY ABOUT US 319
YOUR ROLE IN THE REVOLUTION 320
TAKE A PAUSE, FRIEND, FUTURE HISTORY-MAKER 321
DO THIS NOW, NOT LATER 322
A COACH'S NOTE 323
CHAPTER 20 QUICK REFERENCE 324

CHAPTER 21: THE MOVEMENT SHE LEADS AND SHE LOVES™ 327
WHEN WOMEN UNITE, EVERYTHING CHANGES 327
THE PSYCHOLOGY OF WHY WE NEED EACH OTHER NOW 328
THE HIDDEN COST OF GOING IT ALONE 329
WHAT BECOMES POSSIBLE WHEN WE CONNECT 330
THE SCIENCE BEHIND SISTERHOOD 331
FINDING YOUR HOME IN THE MOVEMENT 331
THE INVITATION TO YOUR NEXT CHAPTER 332
THE RIPPLE EFFECT OF YOUR YES 334
THIS IS HOW WE CHANGE THE WORLD 334
YOUR NEXT MOVE 335
A COACH'S NOTE 335
CHAPTER 21 QUICK REFERENCE 336

YOUR NEXT STEPS 339
YOUR AI-POWERED FUTURE STARTS NOW 339
THE CHOICE BEFORE YOU 339
THE TRUTH ABOUT THIS MOMENT 340
YOUR NEXT STEPS (KEEP IT SIMPLE) 341
    Join the Movement 341
YOUR SISTERS ARE WAITING 341
UNTIL WE MEET 342

PREFACE: A NOTE FROM T. RENEÉ

> *"What if AI isn't here to disrupt your life—
> but to elevate it?"*

I wrote this book because I'm someone who always sees the glass as half full. When challenges come my way, I look for the opportunity hidden inside them. When everyone else is panicking, I'm asking, "How can we use this for good?"

So, when the AI conversation started taking over my LinkedIn feed, my email inbox, and even my lunch meetings with clients, I noticed something troubling: All the voices talking about AI were missing the perspective of women like us.

The tech bros were talking about disruption and optimization. The doomsday prophets were predicting we'd all be replaced by robots. The business gurus were obsessing over competitive advantage and market domination.

But who was talking about using AI to be present at your kid's games instead of mentally writing tomorrow's presentation? Who was discussing how AI could help you support your aging parents without losing your mind? Who was exploring how AI could deepen your prayer life, save your marriage from the "roommate syndrome," or help you remember what peace feels like?

These conversations weren't happening. That's when I knew I had to write this book.

For years, I've been on this journey to create what I call the "AND Life," that mythical place where success doesn't require sacrifice your health, where you can build generational wealth while being present for generational memories.

During this journey, AI became the most unexpected blessing. And friend, when I say unexpected, I mean it. I spent weeks with browser tabs open trying to understand it all. I created an AI avatar that looked like I was having an allergic reaction. I tested approximately 837 tools (okay, maybe 25, but it felt like 837).

But through all that chaos, I discovered something profound: AI didn't make me less human; it gave me space to BE human again.

I know you've heard all the scary stories: AI is going to steal our jobs and leave us broke. It's anti-God technology that threatens our souls. Nobody will need real relationships anymore. We'll all become lazy couch potatoes with Humanoid Robot servants.

I understand change is scary, especially when it feels like everything's moving at warp speed while you're still trying to understand why "the cloud" has your photos but your phone says it's full

But here's what I've discovered through my own messy, imperfect journey:

These fears assume we're helpless victims of technology, instead of the wise, resourceful women who've been adapting and overcoming since forever.

What if instead of running from AI, we learned to make it work for us? What if AI could help us become MORE of who God created us to be—not less?

Through my work coaching successful women (you know, the ones who look like they have it all together on Instagram but eat cereal for dinner because they're too exhausted to cook), I've had hundreds of raw, honest conversations with leaders who are secretly struggling:

- Looking successful at the company dinner while feeling like a failure at the family dinner
- Crushing their revenue goals while their health goals collect dust
- Supporting everyone else's dreams while their own sit in a journal somewhere
- Building enviable lives that honestly, they're too exhausted to enjoy

These women were craving something different. A new conversation about AI—one designed for their actual lives, not their LinkedIn profiles. One that came with a strategy, not just more tools to figure out.

This book is that conversation.

It's written by a woman who's cried in her car between meetings, for women who know that struggle. It's about using AI not to become some efficient robot, but to reclaim your time for what matters. It's about leveraging technology while keeping your heart, soul, and sanity intact.

This isn't about replacing your beautiful, messy humanity with artificial intelligence. It's about using artificial intelligence to protect and preserve that humanity.

In these pages, you'll discover how AI can support you as a whole woman—not just the professional you, but the mama you, the wife you, the daughter you, the friend you, the dreamer you.

You'll learn strategies that work with your values, not against them. You'll meet women who were just as skeptical as you are right now, who are now using AI to transform their daily reality.

You'll also discover two powerful frameworks that will change how you approach AI forever:

The **T.I.M.E. Human-Centered AI™ Strategy Framework** for your personal life—a strategic approach that helps you:

Target your true needs
Integrate with intention
Measure what matters, and
Evolve your ecosystem.

No more random tool collecting. Just clear strategy for real transformation.

The **G.U.I.D.E. Framework for Human-Centered AI™ Transformation** for organizational leadership—because if you're leading others, you need to know how to:

Gauge readiness
Unite vision
Identify opportunities
Develop people first and
Execute with empathy.

These aren't just theories. They're battle-tested strategies born from real women navigating real challenges with real success.

Most importantly, you'll finally—FINALLY—get permission to stop trying to be everything to everyone and start being the woman you were meant to be.

The future belongs to women who understand that the most powerful leadership combines artificial intelligence with emotional intelligence, strategic thinking with spiritual wisdom, efficient systems with authentic relationships.

She Leads With AI is your roadmap to claiming that future.

Welcome to the conversation that's about to change everything—without requiring you to change who you are.

With love, hope, and just enough holy disruption to shake things up,

T. Reneé

P.S. - Yes, AI helped me write parts of this book. No, it didn't write the parts that made you laugh, cry, or feel seen. That's all human, baby. That's the point.

INTRODUCTION

Truth Bomb- I Didn't Write This Book Because I Love Tech

> *"Sometimes the breakthrough you need comes wrapped in technology you didn't expect to embrace."*
> – T. Reneé Smith

I was drowning. And not the dramatic, obvious kind of drowning where people throw you a life preserver. I'm talking about that sophisticated drowning where you're wearing designer heels and a smile while secretly using every ounce of energy just to keep your head above water.

You know what I mean, right?

Drowning in the constant pressure to do it all, be it all, and somehow make it look effortless. Building a business during naptime. Trying to be a Proverbs 31 wife when you feel more like a Proverbs 3.1 woman (barely keeping it together). Caring for aging parents while raising kids. And through it all, posting inspirational quotes on Instagram like you've got life figured out.

The struggle? Beyond real.

Something clicked during school pickup. There I was, tenth in the carpool line, simultaneously answering client texts, rescheduling a canceled meeting, and trying to remember if I'd moved the laundry to the dryer. My phone suggested an AI-generated response to a client's urgent question, and for the first time, instead of dismissing it, I actually paid attention. Suddenly I realized, this technology wasn't another thing trying to compete for my attention, it was offering to carry some of the load I was drowning under.

Every single day, I talk to women who are slaying it professionally while feeling unfilled personally. Women who are resisting AI because they think it's one more thing they need to master. Women who are already exhausted and now feel like they're falling behind in the "AI revolution."

Friend, there IS another way. And it starts with completely changing how you think about artificial intelligence.

My Mama Bear Moment With AI

I'll never forget the conversation that cracked my world wide open. It was late—that hour when you should be sleeping but you're up researching everything that's worrying you.

My neurodiverse son was struggling at school. Social situations were hard. Friendships were non-existent. Social Studies was overwhelming. And I was doing what we mamas do—frantically googling, reading forums, bookmarking articles, trying to become an overnight expert in something I didn't fully understand.

I was overwhelmed, emotional, and honestly, I was frustrated. Frustrated that with all my resources, I still felt helpless to help my baby.

On a whim (okay, desperation), I decided to try something, I asked AI for help.

I poured out everything—his challenges, his beautiful strengths, his interests. I asked for research, strategies, scripts for talking to teachers, and ideas for building his confidence.

What happened next made me ugly cry (the kind where you're grateful you're alone).

Instead of cold, robotic responses, I got thoughtful, personalized suggestions. Strategies I'd never considered. Resources from experts I didn't know existed. Questions that helped me see my son's challenges from new angles.

But more than the information, I felt **seen**. Supported. Like I finally had a thinking partner at 10:07 PM who wouldn't judge me for not having all the answers.

That night, I didn't just discover an AI tool. I discovered what it meant to have intelligent support that amplified my mama wisdom instead of replacing it.

Why I'm Your Guide Through This AI Revolution

Let me be real with you about something: I'm not writing this book because I'm some tech genius who's always been ahead of the curve. I'm writing it because I'm a woman who's had to reinvent herself more times than I can count—and I've learned that pivoting isn't just a business skill, it's a life skill.

When my business filed bankruptcy, I had to pivot from shame to strategy.

When the housing market crashed and took my family's construction business with it, I had to pivot from legacy to innovation.

INTRODUCTION

When I went to federal prison (yes, you read that right), I had to pivot from everything I'd built to starting completely over from scratch.

When I experienced three miscarriages, I had to pivot from my dream of the perfect family to embracing the beautiful family God had planned for me.

When the pandemic hit and I lost every single corporate and government client in one day—watching my revenue drop to zero—I had to pivot from panic to possibility.

Each time, I learned the same lesson: The speed of your pivot determines the speed of your recovery. And friend, in this AI revolution, we need to pivot at the speed of AI.

That's why I can guide you through this. Not because I'm naturally tech-savvy (remember that avatar disaster?), but because I've mastered the art of transformation. I know what it's like to face something that threatens everything you've built and choose to see opportunity instead of obstacle.

Pivoting at the speed of AI is exactly what's required of innovative leaders who will guide our organizations and families into this new frontier. It's about being agile enough to embrace change while being grounded enough to maintain your values. It's about leading with both courage and compassion, strategy and soul.

I've rebuilt my life and business from zero more times than most people change their hairstyle. Each time, I came back stronger, wiser, and more committed to helping other women navigate their own transformations.

This AI revolution? It's another invitation to pivot. And honey, if I can pivot from federal prison to speaking on stages across the country, we can certainly pivot from AI-fearful to AI-empowered together.

◆ INTRODUCTION ◆

What This Book Really Is (And What It Definitely Isn't)

This is not a technical manual written by someone who speaks in code and thinks in algorithms. (Thank God, because my brain doesn't work that way and I'm guessing yours doesn't either.)

This is a girlfriend-to-girlfriend guide written by someone who sees AI not as a threat to your humanity, but as a tool for your liberation.

This book is:

- Your permission slip to stop doing everything yourself (finally!)
- Real talk about using AI without losing your soul
- A roadmap for the AND life you've been craving
- Proof that you can be high-tech AND high-touch

This book is not:

- Another thing to add to your already overwhelming to-do list
- A promise that AI will fix your whole life (God and therapy still required)
- Tech bro speak translated into pink fonts
- Judgment for wherever you are in your AI journey

◆ INTRODUCTION ◆

The Women You'll Meet

Throughout this book, you'll meet your new virtual mentors—real women who've walked this path before you. (Names changed because privacy matters, but the stories, 100% real.)

- **Sarah**, the Chief Technology Officer who discovered during cancer treatment that AI could maintain her leadership while she focused on healing
- **Maria**, the Director of Operations who went from exhausted administrator to strategic leader using AI to reclaim her actual job
- **Rachel**, the PR agency owner who transformed her business model after learning AI could amplify, not replace, her expertise
- **Patricia**, the CEO who led her organization's AI transformation by putting people first (and turned skeptics into champions)
- **Lisa**, the executive coach learning to integrate faith and technology in ways that honor both
- **Carmen**, the interior designer who discovered AI could handle logistics while she focused on creativity
- **Denise**, the business leader who learned presentation preparation didn't require weeks of exhaustion

And so many more...

Each woman's story will show you something different about what becomes possible when you stop fighting AI and start partnering with it.

Your Journey Through This Book

- **Part I: The Mindset Shift** - Where we dismantle the fears and resistance keeping you from the support you deserve
- **Part II: AI for the Woman You Are** - Supporting every dimension of your life (yes, including your faith, health, relationships, and that inner voice that needs nurturing)
- **Part III: AI for the Roles You Play** - Because you wear many crowns, and AI can polish each one
- **Part IV: Your AI-Powered Future** - Because transformation is better together

What You're Really Going to Get

Freedom: From the lie that you have to do everything yourself

Time: Like, actual time. For rest. For dreams. For that book you've been meaning to read or write.

Energy: Because you're not wasting it on stuff AI can handle

Permission: To be human, not superhuman

Community: Of women who get it and are doing it with you

Sis, This Book Is For You If...

- Your have outward success but desire inward fulfillment as well

INTRODUCTION

- You want to embrace AI but don't know where to start (and you're tired of feeling behind)
- You're exhausted from choosing between your career/business and your family
- You know there has to be a better way than this constant hustle
- You're ready to lead differently—with both power AND peace

If you said "yes" to any of these while possibly tearing up a little, then welcome home. This book was written specifically for you.

The Movement We're Building

This isn't just a book—it's an invitation to join a movement of women who refuse to accept that success requires suffering.

We're the women choosing the AND life. We're leading companies AND being present for dinner. We're closing million-dollar deals AND maintaining our prayer life. We're embracing cutting-edge technology AND deepening our humanity.

We're proving that AI isn't about becoming robotic, it's about having the support to be more authentically, powerfully, joyfully human.

Welcome to She Leads and She Loves™—where we're rewriting the rules about what it means to be a successful woman in the age of AI.

A Personal Promise

I promise you this: By the time you finish this book, you won't just understand AI—you'll have a strategic roadmap for using it to create the life you want. You'll know how to evaluate any new tool that comes along. You'll lead others with confidence. And most importantly, you'll finally have permission to stop doing it all alone.

Ready to stop drowning and start rising?

Then turn the page. Your transformation is waiting.

> The future belongs to women who embrace both technological power and human wisdom—and refuse to choose between them.
>
> — T. RENEÉ SMITH

PART I

THE MINDSET SHIFT

> *"Your mindset determines your capacity. What you believe becomes your reality."*
>
> – T. Reneé Smith

Okay friend, before we jump into all the AI goodness, we need to have a real conversation about what's happening in that beautiful, busy mind of yours.

After years of coaching high-achieving women, I've learned the technology isn't what's holding you back. It's the stories you're telling yourself about the technology.

I see you drowning in AI articles and videos, each one making you feel more behind. I see you saving posts titled "AI Will Change Everything!" while thinking "Great, another thing I need to master between meetings and meal prep." I see you watching your LinkedIn feed fill up with AI success stories while secretly wondering if you've already missed the boat.

I've been there. And that's exactly why we're starting here, not with prompts and platforms, but with the mental blocks that are keeping you stuck.

Because here's the truth: You can learn all the AI tools in the world, but if you're still operating from fear, scarcity, and that worn-out belief that asking for help makes you weak, you'll never experience the freedom AI can bring.

The Five Shifts That Actually Matter

Over the next five chapters, we're going to transform how you think about AI, success, and your own capacity to thrive in this new world. These aren't just nice ideas, these are the fundamental shifts that separate women who flourish with AI from women who fear it.

Chapter 1 - Shift 1: From AI Will Replace Me to AI Will Partner With Me: We'll demolish that fear that's been keeping you up at night and show you how AI is your partner in reclaiming your time, energy, and sanity. This isn't about being replaced, it's about finding the partnership you've been needing.

Chapter 2 - Shift 2: From I Should Handle Everything" to "I Deserve Support" We'll expose the superwoman syndrome for the scam it is, a trap that keeps brilliant women exhausted and overwhelmed. You'll finally get the permission slip you've been waiting for to build systems that honor your humanity.

Chapter 3 - Shift 3: From Success OR Sanity to Success AND Peace: We'll rewrite those outdated rules that say you have to choose between achievement and wellbeing. The AND life isn't just possible; it's the only sustainable way forward.

Chapter 4 - Shift 4: From Another Thing to Learn to This Is Actually My Strategic Advantage: We'll reframe how you think about the time investment in AI. Your hesitation isn't about capability; you've mastered harder things. It's about seeing AI as strategy, not just another tool.

Chapter 5 - Shift 5: From I'll Figure It Out Someday to My Future Starts Now: We'll move you from perpetual preparation to actual progress. Because confidence doesn't come from reading one more article, it comes from taking one strategic action.

The Truth About Your Resistance

You're a continuous learner. You've mastered complex skills, navigated career or business pivots, figured out things that would make most people's heads spin. So why does AI feel different?

It's not because you can't learn it. (Please. You learned how to keep small humans alive while building a career or growing a business. AI is nothing compared to that.)

It's because you're already juggling so much that the thought of adding one more thing, especially something that seems to change every five minutes, feels like the straw that might break your beautifully dressed back.

You're thinking: "Do I really have the bandwidth for another learning curve? What if I invest all this time and energy and then everything changes again? Can I afford to learn this when I can barely keep up with what's already on my plate?"

Valid questions. But they're based on a false assumption that AI is just another task to manage rather than the tool that could transform how you manage everything else.

What This Is Really About

Let me tell you what's happening beneath all that "I don't have time for AI" talk.

You've built your success on being exceptionally good at what you do. You've earned respect through expertise, relationships through reliability, and results through pure determination. Now here comes this technology that seems to do in seconds what takes you hours, days, or weeks.

That's unsettling. Not because you're afraid of technology, but because you're wondering what happens to your value when a machine can do what you do.

Here's what I want you to understand: AI can replicate tasks. It cannot replicate you. Your judgment, your emotional intelligence, your ability to see connections others miss, your capacity to lead with both head and heart—these remain irreplaceable. AI simply frees you to focus on them more fully.

Why These Mindset Shifts Matter Right Now

The AI revolution isn't coming, honey—it's here. And while you're debating whether you have time to learn it, others are already using it strategically. Your clients are starting to expect it. Your industry is reshaping around it.

But this isn't about keeping up with everyone else. (When has that ever been your motivation anyway?)

This is about something much more important: creating the life and career or business you want, not just the one you can barely maintain. It's about having a strategy for navigating constant change, not just collecting random tools.

How to Use This Section

Each chapter builds on the previous one, creating a complete transformation in how you think about AI and your relationship with it. Yes, I know you want to jump straight to the "how-to" stuff (it's coming in Parts II and III, promise), but this foundation determines whether those tactics stick.

Read each chapter like we're having tea, coffee, or wine (no judgment) and working through your real concerns together. The reflection questions aren't homework—they're conversation starters with yourself. The action steps are intentionally small because momentum beats perfection every time.

Give yourself permission to feel whatever comes up. Resistance? That's information. Excitement? That's information too. All of it is welcome here.

Where This Journey Leads

As you work through these five shifts, you'll notice something shifting inside you. The overwhelm will start to lift. The resistance will soften. The possibilities will expand.

You'll stop seeing AI as another overwhelming obligation and start seeing it as the strategic key to finally having space to breathe.

You'll develop frameworks for evaluating any AI innovation that comes your way, no more tool overwhelm, just clear strategic thinking.

Most importantly, you'll stop believing that embracing AI means sacrificing your humanity and start discovering how it enhances many of the things that make you uniquely valuable.

Ready to challenge everything you think you know about AI? Let's start with the fear that's keeping a lot of women stuck: the belief that AI is here to replace you.

The truth is much more powerful and much more powerful than that.

CHAPTER 1

FROM CHAOS TO CLARITY: YOUR AI AWAKENING

> *"Your AI awakening begins when you stop seeing technology as competition and start seeing it as collaboration."*
> – T. Reneé Smith

The AI Training That Shook My Confidence

Between client calls, I found myself in yet another AI webinar that promised to 'transform your business in 30 days.' The presenter was ten minutes in when my confidence began to crumble.

For two hours, I watched the presenter demonstrate how AI could create entire strategic plans, write compelling proposals, analyze market data, and basically do everything I'd spent years learning to do—only faster and cheaper.

After the webinar, I found myself spiraling down a Google rabbit hole: "Will consultants become obsolete?" "Is AI replacing strategic advisors?" "How to pivot your business or career before AI takes over?"

I'd been attending AI trainings for months, each one making me feel more behind. New AI tools launched daily. Everyone was talking about AI agents like they were the answer to everything. And there I was, wondering if I'd spent years building expertise that artificial intelligence could now deliver in seconds.

My eyes landed on the family photo on my desk, my husband's encouraging smile, my sons' faces full of possibility—and a different thought hit me.

What if I was asking the wrong question entirely?

Instead of "How do I compete with AI?" what if the real question was "How can AI help me focus on what only I can do?"

That tiny shift? My whole approach changed, and I haven't looked back since.

The Real Reason You're Scared (And Why That's Actually Good News)

That knot in your stomach about AI, here's what it's really telling you.

You're not afraid of technology. You've mastered plenty of complex systems. You've figured out how to use all 19 features on your Mercedes while applying lipstick at a red light. You've adapted to more changes than you can count.

What you're afraid of is Irrelevance.

You've built your identity around being the problem-solver, the one with answers, the person everyone turns to when things get complicated. And now there's this... thing that seems to know everything instantly. That can write, analyze, create, and strategize without needing coffee breaks, bathroom breaks, vacation, or mental health days.

I felt it too. That creeping fear that whispers: "What if everything that makes me valuable can be automated? What if I'm replaceable?"

But here's what that fear is telling you: **You're ready for your next evolution.**

Because that fear only shows up when you're on the verge of transformation. When you're about to shed an old identity and step into something bigger. When you're ready to stop being valued for what you can DO and start being valued for who you ARE.

(And let me tell you, who you ARE is irreplaceable. But we'll get to that.)

How This Really Looks in Practice

Let me paint you a picture of what daily life can look like when you stop fighting AI and start partnering with it.

Before AI Partnership:

- 5:30 AM: Wake up already anxious, scrolling through emails before your feet hit the floor
- 7 AM: Rush through breakfast while mentally organizing today's chaos
- 9 AM-6 PM: Back-to-back meetings with no breathing room for strategic thinking

- 7 PM: You're home but only half-present during dinner, mind still at work
- 9 PM: Kids' bedtime feels like another task to check off while you plan tomorrow
- 10:30 PM: Finally starting the deep work that moves the needle

With AI Partnership:

- 6 AM: Wake up refreshed after meditation, knowing AI organized your priorities yesterday
- 7 AM: Actually, taste your breakfast while chatting with family (revolutionary, right?)
- 9 AM-3 PM: Deep work on strategic initiatives because AI is handling routine tasks
- 3:30 PM: Pick up kids feeling present and peaceful, work is handled
- 6 PM: Family dinner with real conversation, not mental multitasking
- 8 PM: Bedtime stories where you're engaged IN the story, not planning tomorrow
- 9:30 PM: Quality time with your spouse, discussing dreams, not logistics and practicing your marriage ministry (Yes, actual conversation and connection beyond "Who's picking up the kids tomorrow?")

See the difference? It's not about working harder. It's about living fuller.

The Work-Life Integration Truth

Here's something we need to get straight: Work-life balance is a myth sold by people who probably have full-time housekeepers.

Balance suggests work and life are on opposite ends of a see-saw, and your job is to keep them perfectly level. Exhausting, right?

Work-life integration is what's possible. Some seasons demand professional intensity—product launches, major deadlines, that promotion you're chasing. Others require family focus—health challenges, school transitions, marriage tune-ups.

AI doesn't create balance. It creates flexibility. When work demands your attention, AI maintains family systems. When family needs more focus, AI keeps professional commitments moving. You're no longer juggling all the balls-you're choosing which ones to personally juggle and which ones to let AI keep in the air.

Sarah's Discovery: When AI Became Her Lifeline

Let me tell you about Sarah, a Chief Technology Officer at a Fortune 500 healthcare company. When I met her, she was convinced AI would eventually eliminate her role—which is ironic for someone in tech, right?

"I saw AI tools analyzing data faster than my best analysts," Sarah told me. "Creating reports that took my team days in just minutes. So, I did what any rational person would do, I tried to outwork the machines."

(Spoiler alert: That's not a winning strategy.)

Then Sarah was diagnosed with breast cancer.

"Suddenly, those 14-hour days weren't just unsustainable, they were impossible," she explained. "I was in treatment, exhausted, trying to keep my team running while literally fighting for my life."

That's when Sarah discovered the truth about AI that had been hiding in plain sight.

"I started using AI to create the quarterly analysis I usually spent days on. But I realized AI could crunch numbers, but it couldn't see what I saw."

The AI identified patterns in the data, sure. But Sarah saw the story behind those patterns. The AI suggested operational efficiencies. But Sarah understood which efficiencies would energize her team versus demoralize them. The AI proposed strategies. But Sarah knew which ones aligned with the company's unspoken cultural values.

"AI became my research assistant, not my replacement," Sarah said. "It handled the heavy lifting so I could focus on what actually required my experience, my intuition, my understanding of people."

During her treatment, Sarah's team didn't just survive; they thrived. Not because AI replaced her leadership, but because AI amplified it. She could review AI-generated analyses from her chemo chair, add her strategic insights, and guide her team without burning herself out.

"Cancer taught me that my value wasn't in doing everything myself," Sarah reflected. "My value was in my wisdom, and AI gave me space to offer it more fully."

What AI Is (And Why That Should Relieve You)

Here's what most people get wrong about AI—and why it matters.

AI is exceptionally good at:

- Processing information at scale
- Identifying patterns in data
- Generating content based on examples
- Automating repetitive processes
- Working without fatigue or emotion

But notice what's missing from that list? Everything that makes you human. Everything that makes you YOU.

AI cannot:

- Feel genuine empathy when your team member is struggling
- Navigate the unspoken politics of your organization (you know, the REAL org chart)
- Make value-based decisions when data conflicts with ethics
- Build trust through vulnerable, authentic leadership
- Understand the difference between what's technically correct and what's wise
- Create breakthrough innovations that require true intuition
- Sense when someone needs encouragement versus a reality check

I hear you thinking, 'But what about future AI?' Yes, AI is evolving at lightning speed. Tomorrow it might simulate empathy, mirror compassion, even predict emotional needs. But here's what won't change: the difference between performing humanity and being human.

Now, let's be clear—there are companies out there treating AI like a weapon for mass layoffs, seeing every human as a cost to cut rather than a soul to support. They're the ones racing to replace relationships with robots, thinking profit margins matter more than people. If that's your organization's vision, this book isn't for them. We're talking to leaders who understand that the goal isn't to eliminate humans—it's to eliminate what exhausts them.

Think about your most valuable contributions at work. Are they about processing data faster? Or are they about understanding context, building relationships, making judgment calls, and leading with both head and heart? That's the magic no algorithm can replicate—because it comes from your lived experience, your soul, your very essence.

The companies that will thrive aren't the ones using AI to get rid of people. They're the ones using AI to unleash people—to free them from soul-crushing busywork so they can do the soul-filling work only humans can do.

The Elevation Principle

Here's the paradigm shift that matters most: AI isn't here to replace you. It's here to elevate you to what you're meant to be doing. Think about it. How much of your day is spent on tasks that drain your energy without truly requiring your expertise? The routine emails. The basic research. The formatting and reformatting. The scheduling and rescheduling. The analyzing and reanalyzing.

Now imagine if all of that just... handled itself (With the proper set-up and training, of course—we're talking strategy, not magic.)

What would you do with those reclaimed hours? Who would you become if you weren't exhausted by 3 PM? What problems could you solve if your brain wasn't cluttered with administrative minutiae?

But here's the real talk: This elevation requires participation. You'll need to strengthen what I call your power skills—problem-solving, creativity, strategic thinking, innovation, and emotional intelligence. The very skills that make you irreplaceable. And yes, you'll need to learn AI tools. Not to become a tech expert, but to become a strategic delegator. Think of it as learning to conduct an orchestra rather than playing every instrument yourself.

The payoff? When you combine elevated human skills with AI efficiency, you don't just get your time back, you multiply your impact. You become the leader who solves complex problems while AI handles the routine ones. You're the one focusing on innovation while AI manages implementation. You're the one building relationships while AI builds reports.

That's elevation. Not replacing your humanity with technology but using technology to amplify everything that makes you uniquely valuable.

Your Work in the AI Age

If the future belonged to whoever could process information fastest, we'd all be out of a job yesterday. But here's the beautiful truth, the future belongs to women who can:

- Lead with empathy while leveraging efficiency
- Make wise decisions when data isn't enough
- Build cultures where both humans and AI thrive
- Navigate complexity with both intuition and intelligence
- Create meaning in an increasingly automated world

That sounds exactly like you, doesn't it?

You didn't get where you are by being easily replaceable. You got there through a combination of intelligence, intuition, relationship-building, and sheer determination that no algorithm can replicate.

AI doesn't change what makes you valuable. It clarifies it.

When AI handles the repetitive and routine, what's left is the irreplaceable: your vision, your wisdom, your ability to connect and inspire and lead.

AI: CHAOS TO CLARITY

I'M DROWNING IN AI INFORMATION AND FEELING LEFT BEHIND

AI BRINGS CLARITY AND AMPLIFIES MY STRENGTHS

> ### 💭 TAKE A PAUSE, FRIEND

Before we move forward, sit with these questions:

1. What story have I been telling myself about AI and my value? Is this story serving me or limiting me?
2. What tasks in my work feel draining and repetitive? What would I do with that time if it were freed up?
3. What unique perspective do I bring that no AI could replicate? How could I offer more of this?
4. If AI handled my routine tasks, what bigger problems could I solve?
5. What would elevation look like in my daily life? How would it feel to work from energy rather than exhaustion?

DO THIS NOW, NOT LATER

Your first assignment is simple but powerful:

Choose one repetitive task you do regularly and research one AI tool that could help with it.

This isn't about overhauling your entire workflow. It's about proving to yourself that AI can be a partner, not a threat.

Some starting points:

- Email drafting for routine responses
- Calendar management and scheduling

- Research on topics you explore regularly
- First drafts of regular reports or updates
- Data analysis or spreadsheet work

Pick something small. Something that wouldn't devastate you if it didn't work perfectly the first time. The goal isn't perfection—it's perspective shift.

A PERSONAL NOTE

I know this might feel like a lot. You might be thinking, "Sure, T. Reneé, but my situation is different. My work is too specialized. My industry is too complex. My responsibilities are too important."

I hear you. And I want you to know that many women who have successfully integrated AI into their lives started with those exact same thoughts.

The difference between those who thrive with AI and those who don't isn't technical skill or natural ability. It's willingness to see AI differently—not as competition, but as collaboration.

You've adapted to many changes that have come your way. You've learned new systems, new platforms, new ways of working. You've grown and evolved continuously throughout your career or business. This is just the next evolution.

And this time, instead of asking you to do more, it's offering to help you do less (once you learn it), so you can be more.

Next Up: In Chapter 2, we're addressing the big lie that keeps capable women exhausted: the belief that accepting help somehow makes you less capable. Get ready to finally receive the permission you've been waiting for your whole life (and didn't even know you needed it).

CHAPTER 1 QUICK REFERENCE

Key Mindset Shift: AI as an elevation tool, not a replacement threat

Core Truth: Your humanity is your differentiator, not your weakness

Action Step: Research one AI tool for one repetitive task

Remember: AI handles tasks. You handle what matters.

> When you stop fighting AI and start partnering with it, you don't lose yourself—you find yourself.
>
> —T. Reneé Smith

CHAPTER 2

THE PERMISSION YOU'VE BEEN WAITING FOR

> *"Just because you carry it well doesn't mean it's not heavy. Give yourself permission to rest without guilt."*
>
> – T. Reneé Smith

The Text That Hit Too Close to Home

My phone lit up with a voice message from Lisa—unusual for her during work hours. I grabbed it between meetings and heard her voice crack: "I know you're busy, but I need to vent. I'm sitting in my car in the school parking lot crying because I forgot it was early dismissal day. Again. I'm managing three major campaigns, my mom's medical appointments, homework help, dinner planning, and apparently, I can't even remember to pick up my own kids on time. I keep thinking I should be able to handle this better. Other women seem to manage it all without falling apart in parking lots."

I immediately called her back.

"Lisa, when was the last time you asked for help with any of that?"

Silence.

Then quietly: "I'm supposed to be strong. I'm a CEO. A wife. A mother. I can't admit I'm overwhelmed."

And there it was. The lie that's slowly draining ambitious women everywhere.

The belief that needing support means you're failing. That asking for help diminishes your strength. That admitting you can't do it all solo somehow makes you less worthy of the success you've earned.

I need you to understand something: The strongest women aren't the ones carrying the most. They're the ones who've learned what to carry and what to delegate.

(And before you roll your eyes thinking "must be nice to have help", stick with me. This isn't about having a staff. It's about having a strategy.)

The Myth of the Woman Who Needs Nothing

We need to talk about this fictional character we've all been trying to play, the woman who needs nothing and no one. She's got it all together. She handles her executive role, manages her household, supports her aging parents, maintains her marriage, raises accomplished children, and somehow still has energy to volunteer for the school fundraiser.

She doesn't exist.

Oh, I know you might point to that woman on Instagram who seems to embody her. The one with the perfect family photos, the thriving business, the spotless house, and the abs. (The abs always get me.)

But behind every woman who appears to "do it all" is either: a) A massive support system you don't see b) A level of exhaustion she's hiding c) A prescription for anxiety medication d) All of the above

The real women I know, the ones making an impact, they've learned something valuable: Accepting help isn't weakness. It's strategy.

Jennifer's Breaking Point Became Her Breakthrough

Jennifer's story might be yours too.

Jennifer is a marketing director at a Fortune 500 company and mother of two teenagers. When I met her, she was the definition of "high-functioning overwhelm." Successful career, beautiful home, kids in travel sports, husband with his own demanding career.

"I was everyone's go-to person," Jennifer told me. "My team came to me with every problem. My kids needed rides everywhere. My husband traveled constantly. My mom was starting to need more help. And I just kept saying yes to everything because that's what strong women do, right?"

(Wrong. But we'll get to that.)

Jennifer's breaking point came during a particularly brutal quarter. She was leading a product launch, her daughter was struggling with anxiety, her son's travel basketball schedule was insane, and her mother had a health scare.

"I found myself making critical marketing decisions on three hours of sleep while sitting in a hospital waiting room, trying to coordinate my son's tournament schedule on my phone," she remembered. "That's when my body just said 'NOPE.'"

Jennifer ended up in the ER herself, severe chest pains that turned out to be a panic attack so intense it mimicked a heart attack.

"Lying in that hospital bed, I realized something had to change. My version of strength was literally trying to kill me."

That's when Jennifer discovered what she calls "strategic surrender", the decision to stop trying to personally execute everything and start building systems that could support her life.

She started with AI.

"I felt guilty at first," Jennifer admitted. "Using AI to help manage schedules and logistics felt like cheating. Like I was admitting I couldn't handle my own life."

But here's what happened when Jennifer let AI handle the logistics:

- Family calendars synchronized automatically (no more forgotten early dismissals)
- Meal planning that considered everyone's dietary needs and crazy schedules
- Automated reminder systems for medications, appointments, and deadlines
- Travel coordination that didn't require fifteen text threads
- Work presentations that AI helped draft, leaving her energy for strategy

"The first week, I kept checking everything manually, sure something would fall through the cracks," Jennifer said. "But nothing did. In fact, things ran smoother than when I was micromanaging every detail."

The real transformation wasn't operational, it was emotional.

"When I stopped spending mental energy on logistics, I had space to actually be present. I could focus on my daughter's anxiety without simultaneously planning tomorrow's meetings. I could strategize on the product launch without wondering if I'd remembered to schedule the dog groomer."

Six months later, Jennifer's team is outperforming every metric, her family relationships are stronger, and she hasn't been to the ER since.

"I'm still strong," Jennifer insists. "But now I'm strong in the ways that actually matter."

The Hidden Cost of Doing It All

We need to examine what this 'I've got it all handled' act is costing you. Because friend, the price tag is higher than that designer bag you justified as an "investment piece."

Your Health Chronic stress isn't a badge of honor; it's a ticking time bomb. The tension headaches, the 3 AM wake-ups, the digestive issues, that eye twitch that shows up during busy seasons? Your body is keeping score, and you're losing.

Your Relationships Being physically present but mentally scattered isn't connection. Your family doesn't need a superhero, they need YOU. The real you, not the depleted version who's physically at dinner but mentally reviewing tomorrow's presentation.

Your Impact When you're buried in tasks anyone could do, you can't offer what only you can give. Your unique perspective, your visionary leadership, your ability to see possibilities others miss, all buried under an avalanche of stuff that frankly, AI could handle in its sleep.

Your Joy Remember her? Joy? She's that feeling you used to have when work felt purposeful instead of punishing, when weekends meant rest instead of catching up, when you looked forward to Monday mornings. (They exist, I promise.)

Is proving you can do it all worth what it's stealing from you?

The Permission Slip You've Been Waiting For

I'm about to give you something you desperately need but rarely receive – complete unconditional permission to stop trying to do everything yourself.

Permission to:

- Use AI for routine tasks without feeling guilty
- Delegate without micromanaging every detail
- Say no to requests that drain your energy
- Prioritize your wellbeing without apology
- Accept that done is better than perfect
- Ask for help before you're desperate
- Build systems that work without you
- Rest without earning it first

This isn't permission to lower your standards. It's permission to be strategic about where you apply them.

What Accepting Support Actually Looks Like

When you release the need to personally execute everything:

Morning Routines transform from rushed chaos to organized flow because AI prepped everything while you were dreaming.

Work Days become focused on high-impact activities instead of drowning in email and administrative tasks that make you question your life choices.

Evenings shift from the second shift of labor to actual presence with people you love. (Novel concept, right?)

Weekends return to being actual weekends, not just weekdays without meetings.

Your Leadership evolves from doing to directing, from managing to strategizing, from exhaustion to inspiration.

This isn't about becoming lazy or disconnected. It's about becoming effective in ways that matter.

The Resistance Is Real (And That's Okay)

I know what you might be thinking:

> "But people rely on me to handle things personally." *Reality check: They rely on things being handled well, not necessarily by you.*
>
> "I'm faster at doing it myself." *Truth bomb: You're faster at staying overwhelmed too. Speed isn't the goal, sustainability is.*

"What if AI makes mistakes?" Wake-up call: *You make mistakes too, especially when you're exhausted. At least AI doesn't get cranky or need caffeine.*

"I should be able to manage this." Real talk: *According to whom? That voice isn't wisdom, it's conditioning. Probably from that same voice that told you sleeping was optional and self-care was selfish. We're not listening to her anymore.*

The Permission You've Been Waiting For

I HAVE TO DO EVERYTHING MYSELF TO PROVE I'M GOOD ENOUGH

SMART WOMEN USE AI TO MULTIPLY THEIR IMPACT

> 💬 **TAKE A PAUSE, FRIEND**
>
> Let's get radically honest:
>
> 1. What story am I telling myself about why I have to do everything personally? Where did this belief originate? (Hint: It's usually not your own voice.)
> 2. What am I afraid will happen if I start delegating to AI? Is this fear based on evidence or assumption?
> 3. Where in my life am I performing strength instead of practicing wisdom? What would wisdom look like instead?
> 4. What could I create if I had 10 hours back each week? Not what I should do, what I WANT to do.
> 5. Who benefits from me being exhausted? Seriously. Name them. I'll wait.

DO THIS NOW, NOT LATER

Your assignment is different from Chapter 1. This time, we're going deeper:

Create Your "Stop Doing" List

1. List 10 things you regularly do that drain your energy
2. Circle the 3 that take the most time

3. For each circled item, ask:
    - Does this require my unique expertise?
    - Could AI handle this with proper setup?
    - What would I do with this reclaimed time?
4. Choose ONE to experiment with delegating to AI this week
5. Notice any guilt or resistance that comes up, that's information about your beliefs

Some examples to get you started:

- Creating social media content calendars
- Writing thank-you notes and follow-up messages
- Coordinating volunteer schedules for kids' activities
- Tracking and categorizing business expenses
- Comparing vendor quotes and pricing options
- Building PowerPoint decks from your content
- Performing research for an RFP proposal response

The goal isn't to delegate everything. It's to prove to yourself that delegation doesn't mean you're dropping the ball.

The Ripple Effect of Your Permission

When you give yourself permission to accept support, you don't just change your life. You change the lives of those around you.

Your kids see that strength includes knowing when to ask for help. (Imagine that—modeling healthy boundaries for the next generation.)

Your team learns that leadership means leveraging resources, not hoarding responsibilities.

Your friends feel permission to admit their own overwhelm instead of pretending everything's "fine."

Your industry starts questioning whether burnout is really the price of success.

Most importantly, you become living proof that there's another way.

A PERSONAL NOTE

You are not weak for needing support. You are not failing because you can't do it all, that's humanly impossible. You are not less valuable because you choose tools over torture.

The world doesn't need another exhausted woman trying to prove she's superhuman. The world needs women who are rested, resourced, and operating from their zone of genius instead of their zone of endurance.

That woman who's trying to hold it all together, all by herself? She's not inspiring, she's heartbreaking. Because she's choosing to suffer when support is available.

You deserve better than sophisticated suffering. You deserve systems that support your success without stealing your soul.

And beautiful friend, that starts with giving yourself permission to accept help, even if that help comes with artificial intelligence.

Next Up: In Chapter 3, we're going to blow up the biggest lie about success—that you have to choose between achievement and happiness. Get ready to discover what becomes possible when you refuse to accept either/or and insist on both/and.

CHAPTER 2 QUICK REFERENCE

Key Mindset Shift: From "I should handle everything" to "I choose my focus wisely"

Core Truth: Strategic delegation is leadership, not weakness

Action Step: Create your "Stop Doing" list and delegate one task to AI

Remember: The strongest women build the best support systems.

> " Your version of strength shouldn't require suffering.

— T. Reneé Smith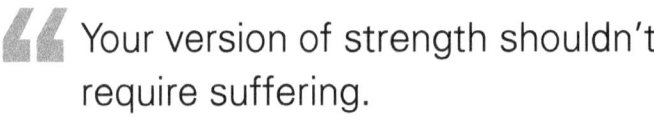

CHAPTER 3

FROM EITHER/OR TO EVERYTHING

> *"Success without peace is just sophisticated suffering."*
> – T. Reneé Smith

When My Husband Called Me Out

It was a Sunday afternoon, and my husband and I were having what started as a casual conversation over dinner. You know, one of those rare moments when the house was quiet and we had time to talk.

"Can I be honest about something?" he asked, with that tone that made me put down my fork.

"Your family gets your leftovers," he said gently but directly. "Your business gets your best energy, your focused attention, your creative ideas. But by the time you get to us, you're running on fumes."

I started to defend myself—listing all the things I did for our family, all the ways I showed up. But he wasn't finished.

"I'm not questioning your love. I'm questioning your priorities. Because if something doesn't shift in how you're approaching success, you're going to end up being a single mother—not because I want to leave, but because there won't be a marriage left to save."

That hit different.

Because he was right. I'd been so focused on building something to leave FOR my family that I'd forgotten to BE with my family. I was winning at business and losing at life.

That's when I understood: Success without peace isn't success at all. It's just sophisticated suffering with an impressive LinkedIn profile.

The "OR" Life Lie

We've been sold a massive lie about what success looks like, especially as women leaders and CEOs. The lie says life is a series of either/or choices:

> **Either** you build a thriving business/career **OR** you have a connected family
>
> **Either** you hit seven figures **OR** you have seven hours of sleep
>
> **Either** you scale your company **OR** you scale back your dreams
>
> **Either** you're a powerful CEO/leader **OR** you're a present mother
>
> **Either** you lead with excellence **OR** you live with ease

This is the "OR" life and honestly, it's exhausting.

The "OR" life has you believing that every win in business or your career requires a loss at home. That every moment spent on self-care is a moment stolen from success. That wanting both achievement and happiness makes you greedy or unrealistic.

But what if the most successful women you know have figured out something different? What if they're living the "AND" life instead?

Meet the AND Life

The AND life is a completely different paradigm. It's the radical idea that you don't have to choose between the things that matter most. That you can be both successful and sane. That you can build wealth while building relationships. That you can lead an empire and love your life.

The AND life looks like:

- Closing million-dollar deals AND making it to bedtime stories
- Scaling your company AND maintaining your marriage
- Leading a team AND taking care of your health
- Building generational wealth AND creating generational memories
- Being respected in boardrooms AND being present in living rooms

This isn't about "having it all" in that impossible, do-everything-perfectly way. It's about having what matters most to YOU—strategically, intentionally, unapologetically.

Maria's AND Life Revolution

Maria runs a social impact company that just crossed $15 million in revenue. When I first met her, she was the poster child for 'successful but suffocating'.

"I was winning all the awards," Maria told me. "Entrepreneur of the Year, Top 40 Under 40, you name it. But I was losing everything that mattered. My daughter literally scheduled meetings with me through my assistant because it was the only way to get my attention."

The wake-up call came when Maria's mother was diagnosed with Alzheimer's.

"I realized my definition of success was completely broken," she said. "I was about to miss the last coherent years with the woman who made me who I am."

That's when Maria decided to stop living the "OR" life and design her own "AND" life. But here's the key, she didn't do it by working harder. She did it by working differently.

With AI support, Maria did some major restructuring:

- Routine business operations automated, freeing her from daily firefighting
- Meeting scheduling that protects family time—no exceptions
- AI assistance for navigating her mother's health journey
- Strategic thinking time blocked and protected
- Family rituals prioritized like board meetings

"I'm not doing less," Maria explains. "I'm doing it differently. AI handles a lot of my repetitive operations so I can handle what matters—vision, relationships, presence."

Today? Revenue's up, her daughter calls her just to chat, and every week includes sacred teatime with her mom—moments she'll never get back.

The New Success Metrics

If you're going to live the AND life, you need to measure different things:

Energy ROI
Not just "What did I accomplish?" but "How sustainable was it?"

Presence Quality
Being 100% focused for 4 hours beats being 50% distracted for 8.

Relationship Revenue
Are your key relationships growing stronger or slowly dying?

Joy Quotient
What's the point of success if you're too miserable to enjoy it?

Values Alignment
Are your daily actions reflecting what you say matters most?

The Fear That Keeps Us Stuck

I know what you're thinking: "But T. Reneé, if I'm not grinding 24/7, won't I fall behind?"

Let me ask you something: Behind what? The burnout Olympics? The "who can sacrifice more" competition?

Here's what I've learned from studying women who sustain success for decades: The ones who last aren't the ones who burn brightest. They're the ones who learned to burn sustainably.

They understand that:

- Rest is a strategy, not a reward
- Boundaries create freedom, not limitations
- Saying no to good things leaves room for great things
- AI handling routine tasks isn't cheating, it's genius

Your New Success Definition

> 💭 **TAKE A PAUSE, FRIEND**
>
> Time to design YOUR version of success:
>
> 1. What does winning look like for you? Not society's version—yours.
> 2. Where are you choosing OR when you could choose AND? Name three specific areas.
> 3. What would change if you measured success by sustainability, not just achievement?
> 4. Which "successes" feel like failures when you're honest?
> 5. What legacy matters more—the business/career you built or the life you lived?

DO THIS NOW, NOT LATER

Your assignment is to create your AND Life Blueprint:

Week 1: Define Your Non-Negotiables

- 3 business/professional achievements that truly matter
- 3 personal experiences you refuse to miss
- 1 daily practice that keeps you centered

Week 2: Design Your Ideal Week

- Map out a week that includes both achievement AND enjoyment
- Use AI to handle 3 routine tasks that steal your energy
- Schedule joy like you schedule meetings (yes, really)

Week 3: Test Your New Success Metrics

- Track energy, not just hours
- Measure presence, not just productivity
- Notice what makes you feel successful

The goal? Discover for yourself that the AND life isn't just possible, it's more profitable, sustainable, and fulfilling than the OR life ever was.

A PERSONAL NOTE ✉

Friend, I need you to know something: Wanting both success and happiness doesn't make you greedy. It makes you human.

You weren't designed to be a business machine. You were designed to be a whole person who happens to run a business or lead a team. There's a difference, and that difference matters.

The most successful women I know have stopped apologizing for wanting lives that feel as good as they look. They've stopped believing that suffering is the price of success. They've started using every tool available—including AI—to create success that funds their dreams instead of stealing them.

You get to want both. You get to have both. You get to be living proof that success and peace can coexist.

That's not just the AND life. That's the ONLY life worth building.

Next Up: In Chapter 4, we're exploring why women's leadership style makes us uniquely qualified to lead the AI revolution. Get ready to discover that what you thought was your weakness is your superpower.

CHAPTER 3 QUICK REFERENCE

Key Mindset Shift: From either/or thinking to AND possibilities

Core Truth: Sustainable success beats sprint success every time

Action Step: Create your AND Life Blueprint with new success metrics

Remember: Success without peace is just sophisticated suffering.

> You weren't designed to be a success machine. You were designed to be a whole person who happens to lead.
>
> —T. Reneé Smith

CHAPTER 4

WHY WOMEN ARE THE FUTURE OF AI LEADERSHIP

> *"The future belongs to leaders who remember how to feel."*
> – T. Reneé Smith

The Tech Conference That Made Me Laugh (And Then Get Mad)

There I was, sitting in yet another AI conference, wearing my uncomfortable "professional" shoes and trying not to check my phone. The room was packed with executives—90% men—all getting excited about "maximizing AI efficiency" and "streamlining operations."

For an hour, I listened to presentations that sounded like they were written by robots FOR robots. Everything was about cutting costs, reducing headcount, and automating everything that moves.

Y'all, I was bored. And I don't bore easily.

When it was finally my turn to speak, I decided to shake things up. "Quick question," I said. "How many of you have asked your employees how they FEEL about these AI changes?"

You could've heard a pin drop. One CEO chuckled like I'd just asked him to consider his horoscope before making business decisions.

"Feelings?" he said. "We're talking about business transformation here."

"Exactly," I said, channeling my sweetest bless-your-heart energy. "And transformation without considering human emotion isn't transformation, it's just expensive chaos. But what do I know? I'm just a woman who's built multiple successful businesses by actually caring about people."

The room shifted. Because suddenly Mr. Efficiency realized his perfect AI strategy was missing something crucial: actual humans.

And that moment? That's exactly why women need to be leading this AI revolution, not following it.

What's Really Happening in AI Leadership Right Now

The current state of AI leadership is being dominated by people who think in spreadsheets, not souls. Who see every human interaction as "friction" to be eliminated. Who get geeked about gigabytes but glazed over when you mention actual people.

Listen, I'm all for efficiency. I love a streamlined process as much as the next CEO. But when efficiency becomes your only love language, here's what happens:

- You get those customer service bots that have you yelling "REPRESENTATIVE!" into your phone like a crazy person

- Your best employees start "exploring new opportunities" (aka updating LinkedIn before lunch) because they feel replaceable

- You invest in fancy AI tools that work perfectly in the demo but have your team secretly using spreadsheets again by week three

- You create "solutions" that solve problems nobody had while ignoring the ones keeping people up at night

I've seen too many companies optimize their humanity right out of the building. They've got all the tech but none of the trust. All the automation but none of the admiration from their teams.

What's missing? The kind of leadership women have been delivering since day one—we just haven't been getting the credit (or the budgets) for it.

Your "Soft Skills" Are Actually Superpowers (And I'm Tired of Pretending They're Not)

Let's talk about those qualities that have been dismissed as "soft skills" your entire career. You know, the ones that never make it onto your performance review but somehow make everything work?

Time for a reframe.

Emotional Intelligence

While others are asking "How fast can AI do this?" you're asking "Is this actually helpful or just impressive?" You naturally consider how changes feel, not just how they function.

Big-Picture Thinking

Men often see AI as a tool for specific tasks. You see the ripple effects—how it impacts your team's confidence, your customer's experience, your kids' future. You think in connections, not compartments.

Relationship Building

You understand that the fanciest technology in the world fails without buy-in. You build bridges where others build walls. You get people excited about change instead of resistant to it.

That Gut Feeling

You know that feeling when something looks perfect on paper but feels wrong in your spirit? That's not being "too emotional." That's pattern recognition at a level AI wishes it could achieve.

Playing the Long Game

While others chase this quarter's numbers, you're thinking about the world you're leaving for your grandbabies. You ask, "What kind of future are we creating?" (And then you care about the answer.)

Values-Driven Decisions

You don't just ask "Can we?" You ask "Should we?" And in the age of AI, that question could literally save humanity from itself.

These aren't soft skills. These are THE skills that determine whether AI becomes our best tool or our biggest regret.

Sarah's Story: When Heart Meets Hard Data

Remember Sarah from Chapter 1? When she brought her whole self to AI leadership after cancer treatment, something powerful happened.

After cancer treatment, Sarah was put in charge of implementing AI in patient care. The board wanted maximum efficiency. The tech team wanted to automate everything that wasn't nailed down.

But Sarah had just lived the patient experience. She knew what "efficient" healthcare felt like when you're scared and sick.

"Everyone was obsessed with reducing call times," Sarah told me. "But I kept thinking about my chemo days, sitting in that chair, just needing someone to tell me I wasn't crazy for being terrified."

Sarah designed something revolutionary (only revolutionary because it included common sense). Yes, the AI handles appointments and prescription refills. But it also recognizes emotional cues. When a patient sounds distressed, confused, or just lonely, the system instantly connects them to a real human.

"My male colleagues said I was 'compromising ROI' by keeping humans in the loop," Sarah laughs. "Until our patient satisfaction scores went through the roof and our nurse's attrition rate was reduced. Turns out, when you design AI for actual humans instead of theoretical users, magic happens."

Why AI Desperately Needs Women's Leadership

Here's something that should keep every CEO up at night: AI systems learn from their creators. And right now, most AI is being created by teams that look nothing like the world they're serving.

We've already seen AI that:

- Automatically assumes nurses are women and doctors are men
- Offers women lower credit limits than men with identical finances
- Fails to identify people of color accurately (but never misses someone who looks like the developers)
- Flags career gaps without considering they might be for caregiving
- Predicts 'culture fit' based on who went to what schools

This isn't just harmful, it's expensive. AI that only works for some people is AI that fails. Period.

The Power of Involving Women in the AI Conversation

When women are involved in AI development, everyone wins because we naturally consider:

- How this affects different types of people (not just the 'average user' who somehow always fits one narrow profile)
- What could go wrong in the real world (not just in the perfect demo)
- How this feels to use, not just how it functions
- Whether our grandmothers could figure it out
- If this makes life better or just more complicated

What Changes When Women Lead AI

When women take the lead on AI initiatives, the entire conversation shifts:

Instead of "Move fast and break things"
We say "Move thoughtfully and build things that last"

Instead of "Minimize human involvement"
We say "Maximize human potential"

Instead of "What will this eliminate?"
We ask "What will this enable?"

Instead of "Trust the data"
We say "Trust the data AND your intuition"

Instead of "Disrupt everything"
We consider "Enhance what's working"

And before you think this makes us less innovative, creating AI that works for everyone IS the innovation.

But What If I'm Not Technical?

Stop right there. I know what you're thinking: "But T. Reneé, I still ask my kids for tech help. How can I lead AI initiatives?"

Friend, can I be real with you? I'm out here teaching AI strategies and I still text my son asking how to stop my phone from autocorrecting perfectly good words into absolute nonsense. Last week it changed "AI strategy" to "AL tragedy"—which felt like a sign until I realized it was just my phone being dramatic.

But guess what? I can still transform businesses with AI because technical perfection isn't the point—strategic thinking is.

The tech folks have technical covered. What they DON'T have—what they desperately NEED—is someone who understands:

- Why that 'efficient' chatbot has customers wanting to throw their phone
- How to get your team excited about AI instead of terrified
- When human connection matters more than automated efficiency
- What questions to ask before implementing something you can't undo
- How to spot bias in systems before it becomes a lawsuit

You've been leading complex initiatives your whole professional life. AI is just another one—except this time, your 'soft skills' are the secret sauce everyone's missing.

Why Women Are the Future of AI Leadership

> 💭 **TAKE A PAUSE, FRIEND**
>
> Let's get clear on your unique value:
>
> 1. What perspectives do I bring to AI conversations that might be missing?
> 2. What have I noticed about technology implementations that didn't consider the human element?

3. How could my leadership style create better AI outcomes for everyone?
4. What concerns do I have about AI that I've been hesitant to voice?
5. If more women were leading AI initiatives, what would be different?

DO THIS NOW, NOT LATER

Time to step into your AI leadership power. Choose one:

The Meeting Move

Next time AI comes up in a meeting, ask one human-centered question:

- How will our team feel about this change?
- What support will people need to succeed with this?
- Have we considered how this impacts different groups?

The Coffee Chat

Find 2-3 women colleagues (you know who they are—the ones who see what others miss) and meet up virtually or in person to discuss:

- Which "human moments" in your work should never be automated
- How AI could amplify your team's strengths instead of replacing them
- What bias or blind spots you've already spotted in AI tools

The LinkedIn Leadership

Share one authentic thought about AI leadership:

- Why your "soft skills" are actually AI superpowers
- A time when human intuition beat data-driven decisions
- Why empathy should drive AI implementation, not just efficiency

Remember: You don't need to become a coding genius. You need to be exactly who you are, someone who remembers that organizations are made of humans, not algorithms.

A PERSONAL NOTE

The fact that you're wondering if you're qualified to lead AI initiatives shows exactly why you should be. That humility, that thoughtfulness, that consideration—that's what real leadership looks like.

The world doesn't need more AI leaders who are 100% confident they have all the answers. We need leaders who ask better questions. Who think about consequences. Who remember that every data point represents someone's mom, daughter, friend.

That's you. That's your superpower.

Right now, people are making decisions about AI that will shape your industry, your children's opportunities, your entire future. These decisions are too important to leave to people who've never considered that efficiency without empathy is just expensive failure.

Your voice isn't just valuable, it's essential. Your perspective isn't nice-to-have, it's a must-have. Your leadership style isn't outdated, it's exactly what the future needs.

So, step up, friend. The future is waiting for leaders who remember that the point of all this technology is to make life better for actual humans.

And nobody does that better than us.

Next Up: In Chapter 5, we're going to build your AI confidence with baby steps that feel doable, not overwhelming. No coding required, I promise.

CHAPTER 4 QUICK REFERENCE

Key Mindset Shift: Your "soft skills" are AI leadership superpowers

Core Truth: AI needs human-centered leadership to succeed

Action Step: Choose one way to step into AI leadership this week

Remember: The future belongs to leaders who remember how to feel.

> Stop apologizing for leading with your heart. In the age of AI, that's exactly what the world needs.
>
> —T. RENEÉ SMITH

CHAPTER 5

BUILDING YOUR AI CONFIDENCE

> *"You don't need to be perfect to get started.
> You just need to begin."*
>
> – T. Reneé Smith

My 100 Failures Before My First Win

Real talk: I quit on AI at least 100 times before it finally clicked. And I'm not exaggerating for effect—I literally had moments where I wanted to throw my laptop out the window.

My husband was the one who introduced me to AI. He kept showing me all these amazing things it could do, and I'd nod along thinking, "Sure, but who has time to learn another thing."

My first attempts? Disaster. I'd ask AI to help me write content for my social media, and it would spit back the most generic, soulless corporate speak you've ever seen. You know the type" leveraging synergies to optimize stakeholder value." Girl, what?

"It doesn't understand me!" I'd complain to my husband.

"That's because you haven't taught it who you are yet," he'd say patiently. "It's like any relationship—it takes time, effort, attention."

I'd roll my eyes. "I don't have time to build a relationship with a computer."

But here's the thing—I was spending hours doing tasks that were draining my energy and stealing time from what I loved about my business. Something had to change.

So, I kept trying. And failing. And trying again. I'd get frustrated when AI would give me responses that sounded nothing like me. I'd quit for a week, then come crawling back when I realized how much time I was wasting on routine tasks.

"Why can't it just GET what I need?" I'd vent.

"Because you're expecting it to read your mind," my husband would remind me. "You wouldn't expect a new team member to know your voice on day one. Why expect it from AI?"

That's when it hit me: People think they're going to master AI in a day. But it's just like building any relationship—it takes time, patience, and a willingness to work through the awkward getting-to-know-you phase.

Once I stopped expecting perfection and started treating AI like a team member, I was training, the whole dynamic shifted. But it took those 100 failures to get there.

The Confidence Myth That's Keeping You Stuck

Let's bust the biggest lie about AI confidence right now: the myth that everyone else "just gets it" while you're struggling.

You know what I see when I watch someone confidently using AI? I see someone who's failed more times than you've even tried. They've just done it when nobody was watching.

Here's the truth:

- Everyone starts confused (yes, even that tech-savvy friend who makes it look easy)
- Everyone's first AI attempts are awkward (mine sounded like a robot who went to business school)
- Everyone still puts in AI "how to make AI sound more human"
- Everyone has that moment of "Am I doing this right?"

The only difference between women who are confident with AI and women who aren't, the confident ones kept going after the awkward phase.

Michelle's Journey: From I Can't to I Teach This Now

Michelle is a financial advisor who went from AI-terrified to AI-evangelist in six months.

"When I first heard about ChatGPT, I literally said 'That's for young people,'" Michelle confessed. "I'm 52. I was still proud of myself for mastering Excel pivot tables."

But Michelle was swamped with client communications, market analysis, and compliance documentation. Something had to give, and she was afraid it would be her sanity.

"My daughter finally sat me down and said, 'Mom, you help people plan their entire financial futures. You can figure out how to talk to a computer.'"

Michelle started small. Really small.

"My first experiment was asking AI to help me explain compound interest to a client who was a visual learner. I must have rewritten that prompt twelve times. But when it finally gave me a beautiful analogy about planting trees, I almost cried."

From there, Michelle built her confidence one small win at a time:

- Week 1: Email templates for common client questions
- Week 2: Market summary translations (from "finance speak" to "normal human")
- Month 1: Client meeting prep summaries
- Month 2: Personalized investment education materials
- Month 6: Teaching other advisors in her firm how to use AI

"The funny thing is, I'm not more technical now," Michelle laughs. "I just stopped being afraid of looking stupid. Turns out, AI doesn't judge you for asking the same question five different ways."

The Real Confidence Killers (And Your Power Moves)

Let's address what's really stopping you:

"It didn't work the first time"

Reality Check: Neither did walking, but look at you now.

Power Move: Every "failed" attempt teaches you how to communicate better with AI. You're not failing; you're training.

"Everyone else seems to get better results"

Reality Check: You're comparing your behind-the-scenes to their highlight reel.

Power Move: Focus on YOUR progress. Are you better than last week? That's all that matters.

"I don't have time to learn this properly"

Reality Check: You don't have time NOT to learn this. How much time are you losing to tasks AI could handle?

Power Move: 15 minutes a day. That's it. Less time than your skincare routine.

"What if I become dependent on it?"

Reality Check: Are you "dependent" on your car? Your phone? Tools aren't dependencies; they're leverage.

Power Move: You're building a partnership, not a dependency. You still make the decisions.

Your Confidence-Building Roadmap

Instead of trying to master everything at once (because who has time for that?), follow this gentle progression:

Week 1-2: The Curious Phase

Start by playing. Yes, playing. Ask AI random questions:

- "Help me write a fun out-of-office message"
- "Give me three ways to say no to a meeting politely"
- "Explain cryptocurrency like I'm five"

Goal: Get comfortable with the conversation, not perfection.

Week 3-4: The Practical Phase

Choose ONE work task that annoys you:

- That weekly report you dread
- Those meeting notes nobody reads
- That data you have to analyze every month

Goal: Save yourself 30 minutes this week. That's it.

Month 2: The Partnership Phase

Now you're ready to collaborate:

- Use AI to brainstorm solutions to a real problem
- Let it help you prepare for an important conversation
- Have it review something you've written for clarity

Goal: Experience AI as a thinking partner, not just a task-doer.

Month 3: The Leader Phase

Time to share your wins:

- Show a colleague one thing that's helped you
- Share a success story in a meeting
- Help someone else get started

Goal: Become the person others come to for AI advice (yes, really!).

The Questions That Build Real Confidence

Forget "Am I doing this right?" Ask yourself:

> *"What's one thing I do every week that bores me to tears?"*
> That's your perfect AI starting point.

> *"If I had a brilliant intern who never got tired, what would I delegate?"*
> That's exactly what AI can be for you.

> *"What would I create if I wasn't drowning in busy work?"*
> That's what's waiting on the other side of AI confidence.

💭 TAKE A PAUSE, FRIEND

Let's get specific about YOUR confidence journey:

1. What's your biggest fear about using AI? Say it out loud (or write it down).
2. What's one task you'd love to never do again? Be honest.
3. How would you feel if that task just… handled itself?
4. What would you do with an extra hour each day?
5. Who could you help if you had more mental space?

DO THIS NOW, NOT LATER

Your confidence-building assignment (and yes, I'm making this ridiculously simple on purpose):

The 10-Minute Experiment

1. Open ChatGPT (or any AI tool)
2. Ask it to help with ONE specific thing:
   - "Create a 5-minute morning routine for busy professionals"
   - "Write a motivational Monday message for my team"
   - "Give me 5 healthy lunch ideas I can prep on Sunday"

3. If you don't love the first response, try again with more detail
4. Celebrate that you did it (seriously, this is huge!)

The Success Tracker Create a note in your phone called "AI Wins" and write down:

- What you asked AI to do
- How long it took
- How much time it saved you
- How you felt afterward

Watch that list grow. Watch your confidence grow with it.

What Happens When You Build AI Confidence

Here's the unexpected gift of becoming confident with AI:

You don't just save time, you save energy. The mental load of remembering everything, organizing everything, creating everything from scratch? It lightens.

You don't just become more efficient; you become more creative. When AI handles the routine, your brain has space for innovation.

You don't just learn a new skill; you model the way forward. Other women will watch you and think, ' If she can do it, so can I.'"

You don't just change your workflow; you expand your influence. And that influence ripples out to every woman watching you navigate this new world.

A PERSONAL NOTE

Friend, I know you might be reading this thinking, "But T. Reneé, I've already got too much on my plate to add one more thing."

I hear you. And that's exactly why AI matters for you specifically.

Can I lovingly remind you of something? You've mastered complex negotiations. Built teams from scratch. Scaled businesses through recessions. Managed board meetings while managing bedtime routines. Figured out international tax law (or at least found the right people who could).

You've been conquering "impossible" things your whole professional life. AI isn't harder than any of that, it's just newer.

And here's the thing—you don't need to master AI despite your full plate. You need it BECAUSE of your full plate. Every minute AI saves you is a minute you can invest in what moves the needle in your business and life.

The difference between women who are thriving with AI and women who are threatened by it isn't intelligence or time or resources. It's simply the decision to start before they felt ready.

You don't have to clear your schedule to learn AI. You just have to be willing to invest 10 minutes today. You don't have to get it perfect. You just have to begin.

You're already beginning. You're reading this chapter. You're considering how AI could lighten your load instead of adding to it. You're closer than you think.

> Your AI confidence journey doesn't start with mastery. It starts with a single question, a simple experiment, a small win that makes you think, "Huh, this could actually give me time back."
>
> What are you waiting for? Your future AI-confident self, the one with more breathing room—is cheering you on. And so am I.

> **Next Up:** In Part II, we're diving into how AI can support the woman you are—not just the professional you, but the whole you. Get ready to discover AI applications you never imagined for your personal life.

CHAPTER 5 QUICK REFERENCE

Key Mindset Shift: Confidence comes from action, not preparation

Core Truth: Everyone starts confused that's normal and temporary

Action Step: Complete your 10-minute AI experiment today

Remember: You've learned harder things than this. AI is just the next one.

> The difference between women who are thriving with AI and women who are threatened by it? The decision to start before they felt ready.
>
> — T. Reneé Smith

PART II

AI FOR YOUR SOUL: SPIRITUALITY, SELF-CARE & INNER WORK

> *"You don't have to choose between being all the things you are. You just need better support for being all of them well."*
>
> – T. Reneé Smith

I was in my kitchen making evening tea (because yes, I'm that woman who loves tea before I wind down), and my teenage son walked into the kitchen with that look. You know the one—half confused, half impressed.

"Mom," he said, "Michael's mom asked what you do for work, and I didn't know how to answer. Like, you run a business, but you're also always here for us. You speak at conferences, but you're at my games. You help other women with their businesses, but you still make our dinner. What are you exactly?"

I stood there holding my tea mug, realizing my son had just articulated something I'd been struggling with for months. What am I exactly?

The old me would have felt like I was failing at something—not focused enough on my business, not present enough as a mom, not clear enough about my identity. But I had a moment of clarity.

I looked at my handsome, thoughtful teenager and said, "Baby, I'm not just one thing. I'm all the things I choose to be, and I've figured out how to be good at all of them without losing my mind."

Then I realized: This is what I want every woman to understand. You don't have to pick a lane and stay in it. You can be the CEO and the room mom. You can be the spiritual seeker and the strategic thinker. You can be the devoted wife and the ambitious entrepreneur.

You just need the right support system to pull it off without burnout.

The 'Pick a Lane' Trap That's Stealing Our Joy

Here's the truth about the pressure we put on ourselves to be one-dimensional.

Society loves to put us in neat little boxes: Career Woman. Stay-at-Home Mom. The Spiritual One. The Ambitious One. The Family-First One. As if we're characters in some limited sitcom instead of complex human beings with multiple interests, talents, and responsibilities.

But here's what I've learned from coaching hundreds of high-achieving women: The most miserable ones are the ones trying to fit into someone else's definition of what they should be.

The most fulfilled ones are the ones who've said, "You know what? I'm going to be excellent at multiple things, and I'm going to get the support I need to do it well."

You know what's exhausting? Pretending you don't care about your career or business when you're passionate about your work. Pretending you don't want spiritual depth because you're focused on business success. Acting like you don't want to be present for your family because you also want to change the world.

You can want it all. But 'all' doesn't mean 'everything at once.' It means being honest about what matters most to you, recognizing that some seasons require putting certain dreams on simmer while others boil, and building systems that support your whole self without demanding perfection in every area. The magic isn't in doing everything—it's in having the support to choose what deserves your best energy right now.

What This Section Will Actually Do for Your Life

In Part I, we talked about the mindset shifts that lay the foundation. Now we're getting into the good stuff—the practical ways AI becomes your personal support team for every area of your life.

Here's what we're covering:

Chapter 6: AI for Your Soul - Using AI to deepen your spiritual practice and self-care (yes, really—technology can support your spiritual growth)

Chapter 7: AI for Your Body - Creating health and wellness strategies that work with your crazy schedule and real life

Chapter 8: AI for Your Heart - Strengthening your relationships and emotional connections through AI support

Chapter 9: AI for Your Mind - Supporting your mental health and emotional well-being with daily AI practices

Chapter 10: AI for Your Environment - Getting your space and systems organized so your environment works for you instead of against you

Chapter 11: Your AI Dream Team - Building a complete support system that makes you feel like you have a personal assistant, nutritionist, and life coach all in one

Each chapter is going to show you how AI amplifies who you already are—your strengths, your values, your goals— without compromising what makes you uniquely you.

The Integration Revolution (And Why It's About Time)

This isn't about adding more to your already full life. This is about getting intelligent support for everything that's already demanding your attention so you can enjoy being the multi-dimensional woman you are.

When AI helps with your meal planning, you can focus on the conversations around the dinner table. When AI helps organize your schedule, you can be present for the moments that matter. When AI supports your business communications, you have more energy for the creative work that lights you up.

You're about to discover something powerful: You don't have to choose between being successful and being spiritual, between taking care of your family and taking care of yourself, between building your business and building meaningful relationships.

You can have the integrated life you've always wanted; you just need the right tools to make it sustainable.

So, pour yourself some tea (or coffee), get comfortable, and let's explore how AI can support every beautiful, complex, wonderful dimension of who you are.

Because friend, you are not too much. You are exactly enough, in all your multifaceted glory. Now let's build the systems that let that glory shine without burning you out.

> **Next up:** Chapter 6, where we dive into how AI can deepen your spiritual practice instead of distracting from it. (I know it sounds impossible, but trust me on this one.)

CHAPTER 6

AI FOR YOUR SOUL: SPIRITUALITY, SELF-CARE & INNER WORK

> *"When you approach technology with spiritual intention, it becomes a sacred tool rather than a secular distraction."*
> – T. Reneé Smith

The Prayer That Started Everything

It was Saturday morning, and I was sitting in my favorite chair for my quiet time before the family woke up. But instead of feeling peaceful, my mind was racing with everything I needed to handle that week—client deadlines, my son's science project, business trip logistics, and about fifteen other things demanding my mental energy.

I attempted to focus on my devotional reading, but honestly, I was just going through the motions. My spiritual practice felt like another item on my to-do list instead of something that actually fed my soul.

In a moment of curiosity, I asked AI to help me with my spiritual practice. I typed: "I'm struggling to find spiritual peace in my busy life. My quiet time feels rushed and distracted. How can I create more meaningful spiritual practices that work with my real schedule?"

What happened next gave me greater insight into how technology could serve my spiritual growth instead of hindering it.

AI didn't give me generic spiritual practice advice or tell me to wake up at 4:00am (thank God, because sis needs her sleep). It also didn't suggest I meditate for an hour while burning sage and sitting in lotus position, because clearly it understood I'm more of a 'sing worship music while folding laundry' kind of woman.

Instead, it asked thoughtful questions about what spiritual practices had felt most meaningful to me in the past, then helped me design micro-practices I could weave throughout my actual day.

That conversation became the beginning of a spiritual partnership I never saw coming, and it's made my faith deeper, not more shallow.

The Both/And Approach to Technology and Spirituality

I keep hearing this idea that you have to choose between being spiritual and using technology, and honestly, I think we're missing something important here.

I believe in digital detoxes. Sometimes you absolutely need to put the phone down, step away from the screens, and create space for silence and stillness. There's real wisdom in that. I do it regularly, and it restores my soul in ways nothing else can.

But here's what I've also discovered: Technology doesn't have to be the enemy of spiritual practice. It can be a powerful ally when you use it intentionally.

I've had some of my deepest spiritual insights while using AI to explore questions I was wrestling with. I've strengthened my prayer life by letting AI help me organize my thoughts and concerns. I've grown in my faith by using technology to study scripture in ways that make ancient wisdom feel relevant to my modern challenges.

The key isn't choosing between technology and spirituality, it's knowing when to use each tool for what it's designed for. Sometimes you need to power down everything and sit in quiet communion with God. Sometimes you need AI to help you prepare for that quiet time so it's more meaningful when you get there.

It's not either/or—it's both/and. And that's where the magic happens.

Meet Carmen: From Spiritual Burnout to Sacred Partnership

Carmen is a 44-year-old mother of three who was experiencing what she calls "spiritual burnout." She'd been leading women's ministry at her church for three years, but instead of feeling fulfilled, she felt emotionally drained and spiritually empty.

"I was so busy helping other women grow in their faith that I forgot to tend to my own spiritual garden," Carmen told me. "My prayer life felt mechanical, my Bible study felt like homework, and I was running on spiritual fumes."

Carmen was skeptical when I suggested she try using AI as a spiritual study partner. "Isn't that cheating?" she asked. Like, am I going to get called into the pastor's office for using technology to understand the Bible better?' But she was open to trying something different.

Here's how AI transformed Carmen's spiritual practice:

Personalized Bible Study: Instead of following generic study guides that felt disconnected from her life, AI helped Carmen explore scriptures related to her specific challenges—parenting teenagers, marriage stress, ministry burnout. AI could explain passages in everyday language and connect biblical principles to her actual circumstances, like how the story of Martha and Mary related to her struggle with ministry perfectionism.

Prayer Organization: Carmen used AI to help structure her prayer time around her family's actual needs instead of feeling scattered and forgetting important requests. AI created prayer prompts based on her concerns and helped her track answered prayers to build her faith.

Spiritual Reading Guidance: AI recommended books, podcasts, and resources based on Carmen's current spiritual questions and growth areas, saving her hours of research and helping her find exactly what her soul needed.

Ministry Preparation: For her women's group, AI helped Carmen research topics, find relevant examples, and create discussion questions that went deeper than surface-level conversations.

The integration was beautiful. Carmen's spiritual life went from feeling like an obligation to feeling like joy. She started looking forward to her quiet time again because it was personalized and meaningful.

"AI didn't replace my relationship with God," Carmen explains. "But it helped me organize my spiritual life so I could focus on the heart connection instead of getting bogged down in logistics. It's like having a research assistant for my soul."

How I Use AI to Deepen My Spiritual Practice

Let me share how AI has become an unexpected partner in my own spiritual journey:

Morning Intention Setting: Instead of rushing into my day, I ask AI to help me set a spiritual intention based on what's happening in my life. Yesterday it was "practice patience with interruptions." Today it may be "look for opportunities to show grace." It takes two minutes and centers my entire day.

Scripture Meditation: When I'm studying a particular verse or passage, AI helps me understand the original context, different translations, and practical applications for my current circumstances. It's like having a theology professor who speaks plain English available 24/7.

Gratitude Beyond the Surface: AI helps me move past "I'm grateful for my family" to specific, deep appreciation. It asks questions like "What did your husband do this week that showed his love in a way you might have missed?" This turns gratitude into a spiritual practice that changes my heart.

Processing Difficult Seasons: When I'm going through challenging times, AI provides a safe space to process my emotions and questions without judgment. I can type in ALL CAPS about my frustrations, use language that would make my mom clutch her pearls, and work through my feelings without traumatizing my family or getting the side-eye from my spiritual friends. It doesn't give me easy answers, but it helps me explore what God might be teaching me through the difficulty.

Prayer for Others: AI helps me organize my prayer life for the people I care about. I tell it what my friends and family are facing, and it helps me create specific, meaningful prayers instead of the usual "Lord, just be with them" that I default to when I'm tired.

AI for Your Soul: Spirituality, Self-Care & Inner Work

Panel 1: MY MIND IS TOO BUSY FOR MEANINGFUL SPIRITUAL PRACTICE

Panel 2: AI HELPS ME CREATE SPACE FOR WHAT FEEDS MY SOUL

💬 TAKE A PAUSE, FRIEND

Before we dive into practical applications, pour yourself some tea and honestly reflect on these questions:

1. What's your current relationship with technology and spirituality? Do you see them as opposing forces or potential partners?
2. Where's the gap between your ideal spiritual practice and your reality? Maybe you want deep morning devotions but you're rushing to get everyone ready, or you crave contemplative prayer but your mind won't stop making lists.
3. If someone looked at how you spend your "self-care" time, what would they conclude matters most to you? Your soul's restoration or just surface-level maintenance?
4. What's one spiritual practice you've abandoned because it didn't fit your real life? And what did you lose when you let it go?

Your answers will help you approach AI spiritual support in a way that enhances rather than complicates your spiritual journey.

Real Self-Care vs. Instagram Self-Care

While we're talking about feeding your soul, can we address the elephant in the room? Self-care has become so commercialized that we've forgotten what it's supposed to do, help us care for our authentic selves, not just our surface needs.

Look, there's nothing wrong with getting your hair and nails done or having a spa day. That's self-maintenance, and it has its place. But let's be honest, a mani-pedi isn't going to fix your boundary issues or help you figure out your life purpose (though it might make you feel better while you think about it."

Real self-care is different. It takes a holistic focus on your mind, body, and spirit, and addressing your deeper needs, not just physical comfort. It aligns with your values and purpose, not just your schedule. It includes your relationships and growth, not just individual pleasure.

AI can help you practice self-care that serves your soul:

Values-Based Decision Making: When you're facing choices, AI can help you consider which option aligns with your deepest values and long-term spiritual goals.

Energy and Rest Guidance: AI helps you understand what kind of rest you really need—physical, emotional, mental, or spiritual, instead of just defaulting to Netflix and wine.

Boundary Setting: AI can help you practice saying no to things that drain your spirit and yes to things that feed your soul, even when the pressure to please everyone is intense.

DO THIS NOW, NOT LATER

Ready to experiment with AI as a spiritual support tool? Choose one practice to try consistently this week:

Option 1: Morning Spiritual Intention (5 minutes daily) Start with: "I'm facing [specific situation] today. My heart feels [current emotion]. Help me set a spiritual intention that will guide me through this day with grace." *Example: "I'm facing a difficult conversation with my teenager today. My heart feels anxious. Help me set an intention for patience and wisdom."* Let AI's response help shape your morning prayer or meditation focus.

Option 2: Gratitude Deepening (10 minutes daily) Stop recycling the same gratitude list by asking AI: "Help me identify five small moments from today that were actually gifts in disguise. Ask me questions that reveal blessings I'm too busy to notice." *AI might ask: "What made you smile today, even briefly? When did someone make your day easier without you asking? What worked smoothly that you expected to be difficult?"* Use AI's prompting to develop eyes that see abundance everywhere.

Option 3: Scripture Study Partnership (15 minutes, 3x this week) Bring your real struggles to AI: "I'm reading [verse/passage] while dealing with [current challenge]. Help me understand what God might be saying to me through this scripture right now." *Example: "I'm reading Philippians 4:6-7 while dealing with financial anxiety. What might God be* *saying to me through this?"* Let AI help you bridge ancient wisdom with modern application.

Pro tip: Start with whichever option makes you think, "I really need that right now." That's your soul telling you where to begin.

CHAPTER 6 QUICK REFERENCE

Key Mindset Shift: Technology is neutral, its spiritual value depends on how you use it

Core Truth: AI can support spiritual practice without replacing the sacred relationship at its center

Action Step: Choose one AI spiritual practice to try consistently for one week

Remember: When you approach technology with spiritual intention, it becomes a sacred tool rather than a secular distraction

---

> Your soul knows what it needs. AI can help you organize the space for your soul to receive it.
>
> — T. Reneé Smith

CHAPTER 7

AI FOR YOUR BODY: HEALTH, FITNESS & WELLNESS THAT ACTUALLY WORKS

> *"Your body deserves the same strategic support you give to your business and family."*
>
> – T. Reneé Smith

The Whole Foods Existential Crisis (Population: Me)

I was standing in the produce section of Whole Foods holding my phone and staring at a display of organic kale like it held the secrets to the universe. Not because I was having some profound vegetable revelation, I was just completely overwhelmed by the sheer number of choices and my own inability to make a simple decision about dinner.

I'd been trying to get healthier for months. I bought all the right groceries, downloaded three different fitness apps, and even invested in those fancy meal prep containers that are currently collecting dust in my cabinet. But somehow, I kept ending up right back where I started: exhausted at the idea of cooking dinner at 6 PM, making whatever was quick, and suffering from what I call "organic fatigue", that special kind of overwhelm that comes from reading every label and second-guessing every food choice.

Standing there surrounded by beautiful produce with labels like "pasture-raised" and "heirloom" and "non-GMO" (because apparently regular tomatoes are now suspicious), I had a thought: If I can use AI to help me run my business and organize my life, why am I still standing here having an existential crisis over whether to buy regular or organic bell peppers?

So right there in the produce aisle (yes, I'm that woman), I opened my AI app and typed: "I'm overwhelmed by all the conflicting health advice. I want to eat better and have more energy, but I need a plan that works with my real life—I'm pescatarian, my husband and sons love chicken, one of my boys is incredibly picky and will basically only eat five foods, I run a demanding business, and I have exactly zero desire to become a cooking influencer. Help me figure this out."

What happened next didn't just change how I grocery shop, it shifted how I think about health as a busy woman.

The Health Information Chaos That's Stealing Our Peace

We need to discuss the current state of health advice. Because honestly, it's completely out of control.

One expert says carbs are evil. Another swears they're essential for brain function. This health expert is pushing intermittent fasting like it's the cure for everything from wrinkles to world peace. That doctor warns it could mess with your hormones. Someone's selling you supplements that promise to change your life. Someone else says they're just overpriced placebo pills that make your wallet lighter.

Meanwhile, you're just trying to feed your family nutritious meals without spending your entire paycheck at the fancy grocery store, find time to move your body between work and carpools, and have enough energy to enjoy your life instead of just surviving it.

Here's what I've discovered: Most health advice treats women like we're either struggling college students with unlimited time and no money, or celebrities with unlimited money and personal chefs. Very little of it accounts for the reality of being a successful woman juggling multiple responsibilities who needs strategies that work in the real world.

But AI? AI can create personalized health strategies that work with your actual life, your real schedule, and your specific goals. Not some Instagram influencer's life, yours.

Meet Diana: From Health Perfectionism to Sustainable Wellness

Diana is a 48-year-old sales director and mother of two who was stuck in what she calls "health perfectionism hell." She'd tried every diet, bought every fitness gadget, and read every wellness book—but nothing stuck because she was trying to follow plans designed for people living completely different lives.

"I was spending more time researching the perfect workout routine than actually working out," Diana told me. "I had several different meal planning apps on my phone, but we were still ordering takeout three nights a week because I couldn't keep up with any of the systems."

Diana's turning point came when she stopped trying to be perfect and started using AI as her personal wellness strategist.

Here's how AI transformed Diana's approach to health:

Realistic Meal Planning: Instead of elaborate recipes that required ingredients she'd never heard of, AI created meal plans using foods her family liked, that could be prepped in under 30 minutes, and that worked with her grocery budget.

Energy-Based Fitness: AI helped Diana design workouts based on her energy levels each day instead of rigid schedules. High-energy days got strength training, low-energy days got gentle yoga, and busy days got 15-minute walks during conference calls.

Hormone-Aware Wellness: When Diana mentioned feeling exhausted despite eating well and exercising, AI helped her recognize patterns related to her menstrual cycle and suggested adjustments to nutrition and movement that supported her hormonal health.

Sustainable Habits: AI broke Diana's health goals into tiny, manageable actions she could maintain—like adding vegetables to meals she was already making instead of completely overhauling her diet.

Six months later, Diana had lost 20 pounds without counting a single calorie, her energy levels stabilized, and for the first time in years, healthy eating felt effortless instead of exhausting.

"AI didn't give me another diet to fail at," Diana explains. "It helped me figure out how to be healthy in the life I actually have, not the life I think I should have."

How I Use AI as My Personal Wellness Team

Here's how AI became my affordable version of having a nutritionist, trainer, and wellness coach all rolled into one:

Morning Energy Assessment: Each morning, I tell AI how I'm feeling physically and energetically. Based on my response, it suggests whether today is a good day for an intense workout or gentle movement, what kind of foods would best support my energy, and how to structure my day around my actual capacity.

Meal Planning That Works: I take a photo of what's in my fridge and pantry, tell AI I have 30 minutes to prep dinner, and it creates recipes that use what I have, taste good, and don't require a culinary degree to execute. It also gives me a picture of what the finished meal should look like. This simple trick has saved me from so many moments of staring into the fridge hoping dinner will magically appear.

Exercise Reality Check: Instead of ambitious workout plans I'll never follow, AI creates movement routines based on my actual schedule. "I have 20 minutes before my next call and I'm feeling stressed" gets me a different suggestion than "I have an hour on Saturday morning and high energy."

Health Pattern Recognition: AI helps me track patterns I'd never notice on my own—like how my sleep affects my food choices, or how certain nutrients impact my afternoon energy crashes. It's like having a health detective helping me figure out what works for my body.

AI for Your Body: Health, Fitness & Radical Self-Care

💬 TAKE A PAUSE, FRIEND

Before we dive into practical strategies, grab your favorite beverage and honestly reflect on these questions:

1. What's your biggest health frustration right now? Is it finding time to exercise, eating well with a busy schedule, having consistent energy, or something else entirely?
2. How much time do you spend researching health information versus implementing healthy practices? And is that ratio serving you?
3. If you could have a personal trainer, nutritionist, and wellness coach who understood your real life and constraints, what would you want them to help you with most?
4. What health habits have you started and stopped because they felt too complicated or didn't fit your lifestyle?
5. How would your daily experience change if you had consistent energy and felt strong and healthy in your body?

Your answers will help you identify where AI can have the biggest impact on your health and wellness journey.

The Real Reason Most Health Plans Fail Women Like Us

A lot of health and wellness advice is designed for people who have health and wellness as their primary focus. But friend, you're running a business, leading a team, raising humans, managing relationships, and probably caring for aging parents too.

You don't need another complicated system that requires meal prep Fridays, Saturday's and Sundays and 5 AM gym sessions. You need health strategies that work with your real life, not against it.

AI can help you:

Work With Your Schedule: Instead of forcing you into rigid routines, AI adapts recommendations to your actual availability and energy levels each day.

Build on What's Already Working: AI identifies the healthy things you're already doing and helps you optimize them instead of starting from scratch.

Account for Your Preferences: Love cooking but hate meal prep? Enjoy walking but dread the gym? AI creates plans around what you like doing.

Consider Your Life Stage: Perimenopause, menopause, post-menopause, high-stress seasons—AI adjusts recommendations based on what your body needs right now, not what worked for you ten years ago.

DO THIS NOW, NOT LATER

Ready to use AI as your personal wellness strategist? Choose one experiment to try this week:

Option 1: Personalized Meal Planning Take photos of your pantry and fridge, give AI a summary of your family's eating habits, then ask AI: "Create three healthy dinner ideas using these ingredients that my family will eat and I can make in 30 minutes or less." Try the suggestions and notice how this affects your dinner stress levels.

Option 2: Energy-Based Movement Each morning for one week, tell AI your energy level and available time, then ask: "What kind of movement would best serve my body today?" Follow AI's suggestions and track how you feel compared to forcing rigid workout schedules.

Option 3: Health Detective Work Track one area where you struggle (afternoon energy crashes, sleep quality, stress eating) and ask AI: "Help me identify patterns and suggest realistic solutions that fit my lifestyle." Implement AI's insights for one week and monitor changes.

Choose the option that feels most relevant to your current health challenges and commit to trying it consistently for one week.

Advanced AI Health Strategies

Hormone-Aware Wellness: AI can help you understand how your menstrual cycle, perimenopause, or other hormonal changes affect your energy, mood, and physical needs, then adjust nutrition and movement recommendations accordingly.

Stress-Responsive Planning: AI recognizes when you're in high-stress seasons and automatically adjusts health recommendations to be more supportive and less demanding.

Family Integration: Instead of separate meal plans for you and your family, AI creates healthy options that work for everyone's preferences and dietary needs.

Travel and Schedule Flexibility: AI adapts your health routines for business trips, busy seasons, and life changes so you don't have to start over every time life gets complicated.

When to Seek Professional Medical Support

While AI can provide valuable daily wellness support, it's important to recognize when professional medical help is needed. Consider consulting healthcare providers for persistent physical symptoms, unexplained weight changes, chronic fatigue that doesn't improve with rest, new or worsening health conditions, or any concerns about your physical wellbeing.

AI can complement professional healthcare by helping you track symptoms for doctor visits, organize questions for appointments, research treatment options to discuss with providers, and maintain healthy habits between checkups. But it should never replace professional medical evaluation, diagnosis, or treatment.

Remember: AI is your wellness partner, not your doctor. When in doubt, always consult qualified healthcare professionals.

CHAPTER 7 QUICK REFERENCE

Key Mindset Shift: Health strategies should work with your real life, not against it

Core Truth: You don't need perfect health habits; you need sustainable ones that fit your actual circumstances

Action Step: Choose one AI health experiment to try consistently for one week

Remember: Your body deserves the same strategic support you give to your business and family

> The healthiest women aren't the ones with the most perfect routines—they're the ones with the most sustainable systems.
>
> — T. Reneé Smith

CHAPTER 8

AI FOR YOUR HEART: RELATIONSHIPS & EMOTIONAL INTELLIGENCE

> *"The strongest relationships aren't built on perfection, they're built on understanding, and AI can help you get better at both."*
> – T. Reneé Smith

The Fight That Taught Me About True Communication in Marriage

Many years ago, my husband and I were having one of those circular arguments that leaves you both frustrated and completely misunderstood. You know the kind, where you're both speaking English but somehow not communicating at all.

I was attempting to explain why I felt overwhelmed by our family's schedule, and he was offering solutions when all I wanted was for him to understand how I was feeling. He was getting defensive because he felt like I was criticizing his efforts to help, and I was getting more upset because I felt like he wasn't really listening.

We went to bed in that heavy silence that follows unresolved conflict (you know the one—where you're both lying there pretending to sleep but are replaying the argument in your heads).

The next morning, still feeling disconnected, I turned to an unlikely source for help. I asked AI to help me understand what had happened in our conversation. I typed: "My husband and I had an argument where I was trying to express feeling overwhelmed, and he kept offering solutions when I just needed him to listen. Help me understand both perspectives and how we can communicate better."

What AI helped me see was a different way of communicating in not just my marriage, but all my important relationships. It wasn't about who was right or wrong, it was about learning to speak each other's emotional language.

The Communication Crisis Nobody's Talking About

Let's have an honest conversation about relationships in our current world. We're more connected than ever: video calls, texts, social media, instant everything, but somehow, we're struggling more than ever to understand each other.

We can FaceTime someone across the globe in seconds. But we can't ask our spouse about the trash without it spiraling into a discussion about everything wrong with our marriage. We have access to endless relationship advice, but our marriages and friendships still feel hard. We're constantly communicating through our devices, but we often feel misunderstood by the people closest to us.

Here's what I think is happening: We've never actually been taught how to communicate well. We know how to express ourselves (sometimes), but we don't know how to truly understand others. We've learned to share our feelings, but not how to hold space for someone else's emotions without immediately trying to fix them or make them feel better.

And here's where AI becomes surprisingly powerful: It can help us become better at the most human skill of all, loving and understanding each other.

Meet Jasmine: From People-Pleasing to Authentic Connection

My client Jasmine, a 41-year-old operations executive and mother of two, was exhausting herself trying to be everything to everyone. She was the friend who always said yes, the mom who volunteered for everything, and the wife who never expressed her own needs because she was too busy managing everyone else's emotions.

"I was so good at recognizing what other people needed that I completely lost touch with what I needed," Jasmine told me. "I thought being a good friend, wife, and mom meant never having conflict or disappointing anyone. But I was burning out trying to keep everyone happy while slowly disappearing myself."

Jasmine's wake-up call came when her daughter asked her, "Mom, what do you actually want? Like, for yourself?" And Jasmine realized she didn't even know anymore.

Here's how AI helped Jasmine transform her relationships:

Learning to Identify Her Own Emotions: AI helped Jasmine practice naming what she was feeling instead of immediately focusing on everyone else's needs. Through daily check-ins, she learned to recognize when she was frustrated, overwhelmed, or just plain tired.

Setting Boundaries Without Guilt: AI gave Jasmine scripts for saying no gracefully and helped her understand that disappointing someone occasionally is better than resenting them constantly. It helped her see that boundaries aren't mean, they're necessary for healthy relationships.

Communicating Needs Clearly: Jasmine kept hoping people would magically know what she needed. Spoiler alert: they never did. Turns out mind reading isn't a love language. AI helped her practice expressing her needs in ways that didn't create defensiveness or tension.

Managing Conflict Constructively: When disagreements came up, AI helped Jasmine focus on understanding rather than winning, and on solving problems rather than being right.

Jasmine's relationships became more authentic because people were finally getting to know the real her, not just the people-pleasing version. Her marriage improved because her husband could finally support her actual needs instead of guessing what she wanted.

"AI didn't make me selfish," Jasmine explains. "It helped me realize that taking care of myself isn't selfish, it's necessary. And when I stopped trying to be perfect for everyone, my relationships actually got stronger."

How I Use AI to Strengthen My Relationships

AI became my relationship coach for important connections in my life:

Marriage Communication: When my husband and I have miscommunications (and we do, because we're human), I use AI to help me understand his perspective before we try to resolve things. It helps me see when he's expressing love in his way even if it's not landing the way he intended.

Parenting with Intention: With two strong-willed teenage sons and an adult daughter, every conversation is an opportunity to truly hear them. AI helps me understand what my kids might be really asking for underneath their questions or complaints and suggests responses that build connection instead of creating more distance.

Friendship Maintenance: AI reminds me to check in with friends during important moments in their lives, suggests meaningful ways to show support, and helps me balance being there for others without losing myself in the process.

Professional Relationships: AI helps me navigate client relationships with more emotional intelligence—understanding different communication styles, managing difficult conversations, and building authentic connections that turn one-time clients into long-term partners.

AI for Your Heart: Relationships & Emotional Intelligence

💭 TAKE A PAUSE, FRIEND

Before we dive into practical applications, pour yourself some tea and honestly reflect on these questions:

1. What relationship in your life feels most challenging right now? Is it your marriage, a friendship, your relationship with your kids, or maybe a professional relationship?

2. Where do you find yourself having the same conversations or conflicts over and over without getting anywhere?
3. When conflict arises, what's your go-to response? Do you shut down, explode, people-please, or try to logic your way through emotions?
4. What would change in your relationships if you felt more understood and if others felt more understood by you?
5. If you could improve one thing about how you communicate with the people you love, what would it be?

Your answers will help you identify where AI can have the biggest impact on your relationships and emotional connections.

The Real Reason Relationships Feel Harder Than They Used To

Here's something I've noticed: As successful, high-achieving women, we often approach relationships the same way we approach our careers or business, trying to be perfect, fix everything, and make everyone happy. But relationships don't work like business projects.

You can't productivity-hack your way to deeper connection. You can't optimize love or streamline intimacy. What you can do is get better at understanding yourself and others, communicating your needs clearly, and creating space for authentic connection.

AI helps by:

Teaching Emotional Intelligence: AI can help you recognize emotional patterns, understand different communication styles, and develop empathy for perspectives different from your own.

Providing Neutral Perspective: When you're in the middle of relationship drama, AI offers objective insights without taking sides or making you feel judged.

Suggesting Better Approaches: AI can help you think through how to handle difficult conversations, express needs without creating defensiveness, and respond to others' emotions with wisdom rather than just reaction.

Planning Meaningful Connection: AI can suggest ways to strengthen relationships through intentional quality time, meaningful conversations, and thoughtful gestures that matter to the specific people you love.

DO THIS NOW, NOT LATER

Ready to use AI to strengthen your relationships? Choose one experiment to try this week:

Option 1: The "Wait, What Were They Actually Saying?" Exercise Think of a recent argument or miscommunication with someone you care about. Ask AI: "Help me understand this situation from [person's] perspective and suggest how we could communicate better in the future." Then, and this is the brave part, have that follow-up conversation focused on understanding rather than being right. (I know, revolutionary concept.)

Option 2: The Love Language Detective Pick one important relationship in your life and ask AI: "Based on [person's] personality and our relationship, suggest three meaningful ways I could show them I care this week that would matter to them." Follow through on AI's suggestions and see if they notice. *Spoiler alert:* they probably will.

Option 3: The "Same Fight, Different Day" Solution You know that one issue you and [insert person here] keep having? Ask AI: "Help me understand the underlying needs behind this conflict and suggest solutions that could work for both of us." Use AI's framework to approach the next conversation about this topic completely differently and see what happens.

Choose whichever option makes you think "Oh God, we really need to work on this," and commit to trying it for one week. Your relationships will thank you.

Beyond the Basics: Advanced Relationship Strategies

Mirror Work: Understanding Your Relationship Patterns AI becomes your personal growth partner by helping you identify how you show up in relationships. Try this: "I notice I [specific behavior] when [situation]. Help me understand what might be driving this pattern and how it affects my relationships." *Example: "I notice I shut down when my partner expresses frustration. Help me understand what might be driving this pattern and how it affects our connection."* AI can reveal when you're projecting, reacting from old wounds, or repeating unconscious patterns.

Emotional Inheritance Mapping We all carry relationship blueprints from our families of origin. Ask AI: "Help me identify which of my relationship expectations or reactions might come from my family patterns. My parents [brief description of their dynamic]." *Example: "Help me identify patterns I might have inherited. My parents avoided conflict by giving each other the silent treatment for days."* AI helps you see what you absorbed without realizing it, so you can consciously choose what to keep.

Navigating Family Dynamics with Grace Family relationships come with decades of history, unspoken rules, and emotional landmines. Ask AI: "My [family member] always [triggering behavior]. Help me prepare responses that maintain my boundaries while preserving the relationship I want with other family members." *Example: "My mother always* *comments on my weight at family dinners. Help me prepare responses that shut down the conversation without creating a scene that ruins everyone's meal."* AI helps you stay centered in your values while navigating complex family systems.

Building Strategic Professional Alliances In business, relationships are currency—but not all connections are worth the investment. Use AI to prepare for authentic connection: "I'm meeting with [person/role] who [context]. Based on their background in [industry/interest], help me identify genuine points of connection and meaningful questions I could ask that go beyond typical business small talk." *Example: "I'm meeting with a potential strategic partner who founded a tech startup after leaving corporate. Help me craft questions that show genuine interest in their journey, not just their business metrics."* AI helps you research and prepare thoughtfully, so when you show up, you can create real connection instead of performing networking theater.

CHAPTER 8 QUICK REFERENCE

Key Mindset Shift: Relationships improve when you focus on understanding rather than being understood

Core Truth: The strongest relationships aren't built on perfection, they're built on understanding, and AI can help you get better at both

Action Step: Choose one AI relationship experiment to try consistently for one week

Remember: AI enhances your natural capacity for love and connection; it doesn't replace the human heart that makes relationships meaningful

> True connection happens when you stop trying to be understood and start trying to understand—including understanding yourself.
>
> — T. Reneé Smith

CHAPTER 9

AI FOR YOUR MIND: MENTAL & EMOTIONAL HEALTH

> *"Taking care of your mental health isn't selfish, it's necessary. It's what allows you to show up fully for everything and everyone you care about."*
>
> *– T. Reneé Smith*

The Day My Therapist Drew Me a Picture That Opened My Eyes

I was sitting in my home office on a virtual call with my therapist, feeling completely inauthentic. From the outside, my life looked amazing, thriving business, happy marriage, healthy kids, beautiful home. But inside, I felt like I was running on fumes and pretending everything was fine.

"I don't understand," I told her. "I should be happy. I have everything I ever wanted. Why do I feel like I'm barely keeping my head above water?"

That's when she shared her screen and showed me what she called the Mental Health Continuum—five colored boxes ranging from "In Crisis" (red) to "Excelling" (green), with "Struggling," "Surviving," and "Thriving" in between.

"Where do you think you are right now?" she asked.

I stared at the screen and had to be honest. Most of the time, I live in the thriving zone, I'm generally happy, performing well, sleeping okay, and enjoying life. But when things get overwhelming and I'm not careful with my boundaries, I can slip into surviving mode faster than I'd like to admit.

"Here's the thing," she said with that gentle but direct way therapists have of calling you out. "You're trying to be a rockstar wife, CEO, mom, friend, and daughter all at the same time. Your superwoman cape is choking you."

She started explaining what each zone meant:

Crisis (Red): Very anxious, exhausted, poor sleep, weight loss, basically when you're wondering if you need more support than your therapist, wine, and prayer can provide.

Struggling (Orange): Depressed, tired, poor performance, poor appetite—when Netflix becomes your closest relationship and you start avoiding phone calls from people who care about you.

Surviving (Yellow): Worried, irritable, trouble sleeping, distracted—when you're managing everything but feeling like you're constantly putting out fires with a water gun.

Thriving (Light Green): Positive, calm, performing well, sleeping well, normal social activity, when life feels good and you're enjoying the ride instead of just enduring it.

Excelling (Dark Green): Cheerful, joyful, high performance, energetic, fully realizing your potential—basically when you feel like you could run the world while simultaneously hosting the perfect dinner party and still have energy left over for amazing sex with your husband. (This is my goal, obviously.)

That visual hit me like a brick. I was basically trying to be Wonder Woman while also being Martha Stewart, Oprah, and Mother Teresa all rolled into one. No wonder I kept slipping from thriving to surviving when life got intense.

Later that week, I asked AI to help me figure out how to maintain my place in the thriving zone and reach that consistent place of excelling. Turns out, even my mental health needs a strategic plan.

What Success Actually Costs Us Mentally

We need to stop lying about what it's really like to be a successful woman in today's world. I'm exhausted from pretending we all have it figured out just because our LinkedIn profiles look impressive.

Here's what people rarely talk about: Being the woman who "has it all together" comes with its own unique set of mental health challenges. You're everyone's go-to person, but you have nowhere to go when you need support. You're achieving goals that should make you happy, but somehow you still feel like you're just checking boxes instead of living.

You know what's exhausting? Being strong for everyone else while secretly wondering if you're strong enough for yourself. Celebrating other people's wins while wondering why yours doesn't bring you joy anymore. Acting like you don't need help because everyone sees you as the helper.

The truth is, mental health isn't just about avoiding depression or anxiety, it's about developing the emotional skills to move from surviving to thriving, with resilience, self-awareness, and genuine joy instead of just constant productivity.

And here's where AI becomes incredibly valuable: It can help you develop these emotional skills through daily practice, personalized insights, and judgment-free support that's available whenever you need it.

Meet Erica: From Beauty Industry Pressure to Inner Confidence

Erica is a 52-year-old beauty industry executive who was caught in what she calls "the youth trap." Working in an industry that literally profits from making women feel insecure about aging, Erica found herself obsessing about every new line on her face and buying anti-aging creams like they were going out of style.

"I was successful, respected, and financially secure," Erica told me. "But I was spending more mental energy comparing myself to my 28-year-old colleagues than actually using the brain that got me to this position. I had a skincare routine that took longer than my morning workout and a medicine cabinet that looked like a Sephora exploded."

The truth hit Erica when she realized she was spending her nights researching the latest anti-aging treatments instead of resting for the strategic meetings ahead. 'I was literally googling 'how to look younger' at 2 AM when I should have been sleeping before my board presentation. The irony wasn't lost on me.

Here's how AI helped Erica shift from external validation to internal confidence:

Childhood Pattern Recognition: AI helped Erica trace her appearance anxiety back to childhood messages received from her dad about how women "let themselves go as they get older" and identify how those old stories were still running her life at 52. "Turns out, my father's voice warning me about aging was still playing on repeat in my head," she laughed.

Daily Confidence Coaching: When Erica caught herself in an aging anxiety spiral, she'd type her fears into AI: "Just saw my reflection in bad lighting and now I'm panicking about looking old in tomorrow's presentation." AI would help her reframe: "Your 25 years of industry experience will command that room, not your concealer. What key insights can you share that only someone with your tenure would know?" This daily practice rewired her response to appearance triggers.

Values Clarification: Erica asked AI: "Help me define what 'looking good' means for a 52-year-old beauty industry executive who's tired of chasing youth." AI guided her through questions like: "When you feel most powerful and respected, what are you usually doing? What do clients comment on—your appearance or your insights?" Through this process, Erica redefined looking good as radiating the confidence that comes from expertise, rather than hiding every sign of experience.

Professional Reframing: When Erica felt intimidated by younger colleagues, she'd ask AI: "How do I position my age as an asset in this youth-obsessed industry?" AI helped her craft her narrative: "While others are still learning from mistakes, you've already navigated many industry upheavals. Your gray hair represents survived recessions, launched brands, and relationships that span decades." This reframing transformed how she showed up in rooms and how she mentored younger women—teaching them to build substance, not just surface.

The shift was beautiful. Erica stopped spending unnecessary time at the dermatologist and started investing that time in self-care. Her confidence increased, her skincare routine decreased to a manageable four steps (down from eight), and she became a more effective leader because she was focused on her value, not her appearance.

"AI helped me realize that my value was never actually in my appearance, that was just a story I was told to keep me distracted from my real power," Erica explains. "The goal isn't to stop caring about how you look; it's to stop letting appearance anxiety control your life and limit your potential. Plus, I'm pretty sure my skin looks better now that I'm not stressing about it constantly."

How I Use AI for Daily Mental Wellness

AI became my personal mental health concierge—like having a therapist, life coach, and wise best friend all rolled into one app that never judges me for eating an omelet for dinner:

Morning Mental Weather Report: Each morning, I check in with AI about where I am on the mental health continuum, kind of like checking the weather before getting dressed. "Cloudy with a chance of overwhelm today? Let's plan accordingly." AI suggests whether it's a day for tackling big projects or a day for grace and gentle movement.

The Great Boundary Reset: AI became my boundary setting coach when I realized the problem wasn't that other people were demanding too much, it was that I was offering too much. "You know you can say no to chairing the school fundraiser when you're already running a business, right?" AI gently reminded me. Apparently, "I can do it all" isn't a life strategy.

Perfectionist Reality Check: When my inner perfectionist starts her daily performance of "Everything Must Be Flawless," AI stages an intervention. It's like having a wise mentor who reminds me that "good enough" in most areas allows for "excellent" in what truly matters.

Life Season GPS: AI helps me figure out what season I'm in versus what season I think I should be in. Just like nature has seasons, so does life—spring seasons of new growth (starting businesses, having babies, launching dreams), summer seasons of full bloom (scaling success, active parenting, peak performance), fall seasons of harvest (reaping rewards, kids becoming independent, wisdom years), and winter seasons of rest (recovery, reflection, preparing for what's next). Turns out, trying to have spring energy in winter season is like wearing flip-flops in a snowstorm—technically possible, but not particularly wise or comfortable. AI helps me honor where I actually am instead of forcing where I think I should be.

The best part? AI never gets tired of my questions, never rolls its eyes when I need the same reminder for the third time this week, and never suggests I should "just relax" when what I really need is a strategic plan for my mental wellness.

AI for Your Mind: Mental Health & Emotional Wellness

💭 TAKE A PAUSE, FRIEND

Before we dive into practical applications, grab your favorite beverage and honestly think about these questions:

1. If you looked at the mental health continuum (Crisis, Struggling, Surviving, Thriving, Excelling), where would you honestly place yourself right now? And where do you want to be?

2. What's your relationship with perfectionism? Are you trying to excel at everything simultaneously, or have you learned to prioritize what matters most in different seasons?
3. How do you typically handle stress and overwhelm? Are these strategies helping you move toward thriving, or just helping you survive?
4. What would change in your daily experience if you felt more emotionally balanced, confident, and genuinely joyful instead of just productive?
5. If you had a personal mental health coach available 24/7, what would you want them to help you with most?

Your answers will help you identify where AI can provide the most valuable support for moving from surviving to thriving.

The Superwoman Cape That's Choking Us

Here's something we need to acknowledge: As high-achieving women, we've been conditioned to believe that we should be able to handle everything perfectly all the time. But that superwoman cape isn't empowering, it's suffocating.

The truth is, you can have it all, just not all at the same time. Life has seasons, and different seasons require different priorities. AI can help by:

Season Recognition: Helping you identify what phase of life you're in and adjusting expectations accordingly. New mom season looks different than empty nest season, and that's completely normal.

Priority Clarity: AI helps you get clear on what matters most right now versus what you think should matter or what mattered five years ago.

Boundary Setting with Yourself: The hardest boundaries to set aren't with other people, they're with yourself. AI helps you practice saying no to your own impossible standards.

Energy Management: AI tracks your energy patterns and helps you structure your life around your actual capacity rather than some fantasy version of unlimited energy.

Do This Now, Not Later

Ready to use AI for better mental wellness? Choose one experiment to try this week:

Option 1: Mental Health Continuum Check Each morning for one week, tell AI where you are on the mental health continuum and ask: "What can I do today to move closer to thriving?" Notice how this awareness affects your daily choices and energy management.

Option 2: Superwoman Cape Burning Identify one area where you're trying to be perfect and ask AI: "Help me figure out what 'good enough' looks like in this area so I can excel in what matters most." Practice implementing AI's suggestions for one week.

Option 3: Seasonal Priority Setting Ask AI: "Based on what's happening in my life right now, what should my top three priorities be this season?" Use AI's insights to say no to things that don't align with your seasonal focus.

Choose the option that feels most relevant to where you are on the mental health continuum and commit to trying it consistently for one week.

When to Seek Professional Support

While AI can provide valuable daily mental health support, it's important to recognize when professional help is needed. Consider therapy or counseling when you're consistently in the crisis or struggling zones of the mental health continuum—experiencing persistent sadness or anxiety, thoughts of self-harm, trauma responses, or when your emotional state is significantly impacting your daily functioning.

AI can complement professional treatment by helping you prepare for therapy sessions, track your progress between appointments, and implement therapeutic strategies in your daily life, but it should never replace professional mental health care when it's needed.

CHAPTER 9 QUICK REFERENCE

Key Mindset Shift: Mental health exists on a continuum; the goal is to move from surviving to thriving

Core Truth: You can have it all, just not all at the same time, life has seasons that require different priorities

Action Step: Choose one AI mental wellness experiment to try consistently for one week

Remember: Burning your superwoman cape isn't giving up, it's growing up

> The strongest women aren't the ones who excel in every season—they're the ones who honor the season they're in.
>
> — T. Reneé Smith

CHAPTER 10

AI FOR YOUR ENVIRONMENT: HOME, SPACE & LIFE ORGANIZATION

> *Your environment either supports your dreams or sabotages them. There's no neutral."*
> – T. Reneé Smith

The Tuesday Evening Clean Up Before the Housekeeper Comes

It was 6:30 on a Tuesday evening, and I was looking forward to finally relaxing with some tea and reading a book. But when I walked into the kitchen, I was greeted by what looked like a small tornado that had made itself at home on my counters.

Unopened mail was having a party with permission slips, while my grocery list had somehow split into three different versions—each in different handwriting, as if I'd developed multiple personalities just for meal planning.

My laptop was open with tabs for summer camps, family vacation research, and appointments for doctors. My phone was buzzing with reminder notifications that I'd clearly been ignoring.

And here's the kicker, I was doing my usual pre-housekeeper cleanup. Yes, you read that right. I was cleaning up so the housekeeper could clean up. My husband still doesn't understand this concept ("Why are you cleaning for the person we pay to clean?"), but every woman reading this is nodding along because you do it too. We all do it. It's like some weird universal law of womankind.

But standing there, moving piles of papers from one counter to another in the great pre-cleaning shuffle, I had a moment of clarity: This mess isn't just about my kitchen counter. The clutter in my environment is a direct reflection of what's happening in my head.

Something had to give, and it wasn't going to be my sanity.

I grabbed my phone and asked AI: "Help me figure out how to get organized without becoming one of those people who labels everything including the label maker. I want my space to support my peace."

What happened next didn't just tame the paper tornado, it gave me a different perspective on how our environment either fuels our success or sabotages it, one cluttered counter at a time.

The Mind-Environment Connection

The state of your space is basically a mirror for the state of your mind. And I don't mean that in some woo woo, crystals and sage way. I mean it in a very practical, "when my kitchen looks like a paper explosion, my brain feels scattered too" kind of way.

Think about it: When was the last time you felt completely zen and in control while surrounded by chaos? When did you last make your best decisions while digging through piles of stuff looking for that one important thing you know you put "somewhere safe"?

Here's what I've discovered: We spend so much time managing the mess that we forget what it feels like to be supported by our environment. Instead of our homes being the foundation for our dreams, they become another source of stress we have to navigate.

The truth is: You don't need to become a minimalist monk or hire a professional organizer who charges more than your mortgage. You just need to understand that organization isn't about having Instagram worthy spaces, it's about creating environments that make your life easier, not harder.

And that's where AI becomes your secret weapon for transforming chaos into calm without losing your personality in the process.

Meet Maya: From Divorce Chaos to I've Got This Confidence

Maya is a 41-year-old restaurant owner who suddenly found herself a single parent after her divorce. When her fifteen-year marriage ended, Maya went from tag-team household management to flying solo, while also taking on the full weight of personal financial management that she'd previously shared.

"Divorce is like someone took your life, put it in a blender, and hit the chaos setting," Maya told me. "I can run a restaurant's

P&L in my sleep and manage staff schedules like a military operation, but suddenly I'm the sole person responsible for coordinating two kids' schedules between two houses and rebuilding our family's financial foundation from scratch. The business finances I had down to a science, but personal finances felt like learning a completely different language."

Maya had always been financially savvy, she'd built a successful restaurant business and understood cash flow, budgeting, and financial planning. But divorce had damaged her credit score, split their assets, and left her managing both business finances and the full scope of personal financial planning for the first time. The mental load of carrying it all was overwhelming.

Maya's reality check came when she spent an entire Saturday hunting for her son's baseball uniform because she couldn't remember which of the seven piles of clean laundry it might be hiding in. "I realized I was using my precious kid time playing hide and seek with their belongings instead of actually enjoying them."

Here's how AI helped Maya create what she calls her "single-mom command center":

Financial Recovery Strategy: Maya went from "we handled the personal finances together" to "I'm rebuilding my financial future solo." AI helped her create a credit repair plan, reorganize her personal budget to accommodate single income living, and develop investment strategies that balanced her business success with personal financial security.

Custody Schedule Mastery: Shared custody meant every plan needed a Plan B, and every Plan B needed a backup. AI helped Maya create coordination systems that worked across two households, complete with kid friendly calendars and communication scripts that kept things drama free.

Small Space, Big Life: Moving from a six-bedroom house to a two-bedroom apartment meant every inch had to work overtime. AI helped Maya design storage solutions that maximized function while still feeling like home, not a storage unit with furniture.

Single Parent Safety Net: When you're the only adult in charge, backup plans aren't a luxury, they're a necessity. AI helped Maya create emergency protocols for everything from sick kids to restaurant emergencies, giving her confidence that she could handle whatever life threw at her.

Maya went from feeling like she was drowning in logistics to running her household like the capable CEO she always was. Her kids adjusted well to their organized new normal, and Maya discovered that being single didn't mean being overwhelmed, it meant being strategic.

"AI didn't teach me to be perfect," Maya explains. "It taught me to be prepared. I know how to run a business but learning to apply those same strategic skills to single parenthood was the game-changer. Now when my ex sees how smoothly everything runs, I just smile and think, 'Thank you, technology, for helping me stay sane in the midst of my ever-changing world.'

How I Use AI to Create a Home That Actually Works

AI helped me stop being a chaos coordinator and start being the CEO of my own household:

The Great Paper Intervention: That Tuesday evening revelation led to what I now call "The Great Paper Intervention." I took photos of every pile and asked AI to help me create a system that didn't require a PhD in filing to maintain. AI helped me sort everything into "handle this now," "keep for my sanity," and "why am I hoarding grocery store receipts from three months ago?" Then it helped me set up digital reminders, so important things don't disappear into the paper vortex ever again.

Schedule Coordination Like a Pro: Our family calendar used to look like someone threw appointments at a wall to see what would stick. AI helped me create systems that consider how my family functions, no early morning dentist appointments for my night owl teenager, automatic alerts when we're about to overbook ourselves, and buffer time because "it only takes 15 minutes to get there" is apparently a fantasy I needed to release.

Meal Planning for Real People: I love cooking and meal planning, but don't like going through hours of recipes to decide what I'm going to cook. AI helps me create weekly menus based on what's in season, what my family will eat (goodbye, Pinterest meals that require ingredients I'll use once), and what I can manage with my schedule.

Home Maintenance on Autopilot: AI created systems that prevent my house from staging a revolt. My husband gets friendly reminders before problems become expensive disasters, organized contractor information so we're not frantically googling "emergency plumber" at midnight, and budget planning for improvements that don't require taking out a second mortgage.

The best part? My home went from being another thing I had to manage to being the foundation that supports everything else I want to accomplish.

AI for Your Environment: Home, Space & Life Organization

💭 TAKE A PAUSE, FRIEND

Before we dive into practical strategies, grab your favorite beverage and take an honest look around:

1. What areas of your home make you feel energized versus drained when you look at them? And what's the difference between those spaces?

2. How much time do you spend each week looking for things, managing household chaos, or doing the pre-cleaning cleanup dance?
3. If your environment could talk, what would it say about your mental state? Would it be encouraging or calling you out?
4. What would change in your daily energy if your home consistently supported your goals instead of sabotaging them with hidden time traps?
5. If you could have three areas of your life run on autopilot, what would free up the most mental space for what matters to you?

Your answers will help you identify where AI can transform your environment from energy drain to success engine.

Why Most Organization Advice Doesn't Work for Busy Women

Here's the truth about most organization advice: It's written by people who apparently don't live with other humans, run businesses, lead teams, or have any responsibilities beyond maintaining perfect label maker systems.

They assume you have unlimited time to maintain seventeen different categories of things, unlimited budget for custom storage solutions that cost more than your car payment, and unlimited patience for family members who treat your beautiful organization system like a suggestion rather than the law.

Real life is messier than that. Kids get sick the day you planned to organize the playroom. Work emergencies collide with back-to-school prep. The gorgeous system you saw on social media requires more maintenance than your actual business.

But here's what I've learned: The goal isn't to create a home that could be featured in a magazine, it's to create systems that support your real life with your real responsibilities.

AI gets this because it can design organization that's sustainable:

Flexible Systems: Organization that bends when life gets crazy instead of breaking completely and leaving you feeling like a failure.

Human-Friendly Solutions: Systems that work for different personalities, ages, and energy levels instead of requiring everyone to become organization robots.

Low-Maintenance Magic: Solutions that stay functional without requiring daily perfection or superhuman discipline.

Goal-Oriented Design: Environments built around what you're trying to accomplish, not what looks impressive on Instagram.

DO THIS NOW, NOT LATER

Ready to transform your environment from chaos creator to success supporter? Pick one experiment to try this week:

Option 1: The Surface Liberation Project Choose your most chaotic surface—kitchen counter, desk, that mysterious chair that seems to attract everything. Take a photo and tell AI: "This is my problem area. I tend to [describe your actual habits]. Help me create a system for managing this space that works with how I really function, not how I wish I functioned."

> *Example: "This is my kitchen counter. I tend to dump mail here when I walk in, stack papers I'll 'deal with later,' and use it as command central for the whole family. Help me create a system that works with these patterns instead of against them."*

Implement AI's suggestions and track how it affects your daily peace of mind.

Option 2: The Schedule Sanity Makeover Show AI your current calendar chaos and explain: "Here's our family schedule. We have [describe your family dynamics]. These are our recurring conflicts: [list them]. Help me create a coordination system that prevents disasters and actually considers how real humans function."

> *Example: "Family of four, two teens with sports, husband travels monthly, I run a business from home. We*

constantly double-book, forget pickups, and argue about who knew what when. Help me create a system that accounts for teenage communication styles and travel schedules."

Try AI's strategies for one week and notice the difference in family stress levels.

Option 3: The Paper Trail Solution Gather one week's worth of papers, forms, and random documents. Tell AI: "These are the types of papers that pile up in my house: [list categories]. I tend to [describe your paper habits]. Help me create a simple system that doesn't require color-coded files or a label maker addiction."

Example: "School forms, medical EOBs, receipts, kids' artwork, mail I'm afraid to throw away. I tend to pile papers to 'sort later' then panic when I need something. Help me create a system for someone who will never be a filing enthusiast."

Set up AI's system and measure how much mental energy it frees up.

Choose whichever option would give you the biggest daily relief and commit to trying it for one full week before deciding if it works for your life.

CHAPTER 10 QUICK REFERENCE

Key Mindset Shift: Your environment is either supporting your success or sabotaging it—there's no neutral ground

Core Truth: Organization isn't about perfection, it's about creating systems that make your life easier, not harder

Action Step: Choose one area of environmental chaos to transform with AI support this week

Remember: The goal is progress, not Pinterest-perfection

> The most successful women don't have perfect homes, they have homes that perfectly support their goals.
>
> — T. RENEÉ SMITH

CHAPTER 11

YOUR AI DREAM TEAM: LIVING LIKE YOU HAVE A PERSONAL STAFF (WITHOUT THE CELEBRITY BUDGET)

> *"You don't need a million-dollar budget to live like a mogul; you just need smart systems that make you feel like one."*
> – T. Reneé Smith

The Morning That Made Me Feel Like Oprah (But Better)

I was sitting at my kitchen table feeling like I had superpowers. Not because I'd suddenly developed the ability to fly or read minds, but because I'd just opened my personalized morning briefing that made me feel like I was running a small empire.

After school drop-off, I always check my AI-generated daily overview:

"Good morning! Based on the calendar and weather app data you shared, here's your day: You have two client calls, your youngest son has swimming practice at 4 PM, and there's a 70% chance of rain this afternoon.

Suggestions:

- Move your lunch meeting indoors due to weather
- Consider rescheduling your 3 PM call to 2:30 PM to allow time for pickup
- Your meal prep plan from Sunday is in the fridge (chicken and veggie stir-fry)
- Priority emails to address: small business cohort proposal, team meeting follow-up, vendor contract
- Key talking points for your 10 AM presentation attached based on the outline you provided

Have a beautiful day!"

I sat there for a moment, savoring my tea and marveling at how organized and prepared I felt before my workday even started. Now, full transparency, this took some setup. My amazing assistant and I spent time configuring these AI systems—connecting calendars, setting up templates, training AI on my preferences. But once it was running? Pure coordination magic.

This wasn't because I'd suddenly become more disciplined or hired a team of assistants. This was because I'd learned to use AI like celebrities use their entourages—as an intelligent system that organizes information and suggests solutions so I can make better decisions faster.

For the first time in years, I felt like I was directing my life with clear information instead of just reacting to whatever felt most urgent.

That morning, my perspective shifted: You don't need Kim Kardashian's budget to get strategic support. Yes, you'd need her budget to afford human assistants who anticipate your every need. But AI can give you something powerful—organized information, smart suggestions, and time-saving templates that make your life feel manageable instead of chaotic.

The Celebrity Secret We Can All Access Now

Let's talk about why celebrities always seem so put-together, creative, and present for their families despite having incredibly demanding careers. It's not because they're superhuman or naturally more organized than the rest of us.

It's because they have teams.

Oprah has people who handle her schedule, coordinate her logistics, manage her communications, plan her meals, research her decisions, and organize her life. Beyoncé has assistants who prep her for meetings, handle her travel, manage her household, and filter her information. Even smaller influencers have teams that coordinate their content, manage their brand, and handle their business operations.

Here's what's revolutionary about our current moment: AI can function as your affordable version of that celebrity support team.

AI becomes your personal assistant coordinating schedules with precision. AI transforms into your private chef planning meals and creating shopping lists tailored to your family. AI evolves into your communications manager handling routine correspondence with your authentic voice. AI develops into your research analyst providing insights for both business and personal decisions.

The difference between feeling like you're drowning in your own life and feeling like you're gracefully directing it often comes down to having the right support systems.

Meet Aria: Living Like a Multi-Industry Mogul

Aria is a 35-year-old powerhouse who's building multiple empires across business, entertainment, and social impact. She has a skincare line, a production company, various brand partnerships, plus a husband who travels for work and two kids under 10.

When people see Aria's life on social media, they assume she has a massive team managing everything. The reality? She has a small but mighty team of three people who leverage AI to multiply their effectiveness exponentially. It's revolutionized how she operates across all her ventures.

"People see the highlight reel and think I have this enormous staff, but the truth is I have three incredible people who use AI like it's our secret weapon," Aria told me. "My assistant, operations manager, and part-time nanny all use AI to amplify what they can accomplish. It's like having a team of fifteen with the budget for three."

Here's how Aria's small team uses AI to function like a celebrity-level support system:

Executive Assistant Extraordinaire: Aria's assistant uses AI to create personalized daily briefings covering family schedules, business priorities, and suggested responses for social media engagement. "My assistant feeds our priorities into AI, and it helps organize everything so she can focus on the high-level coordination instead of getting buried in logistics," Aria explains.

Business Operations Manager: Her operations person uses AI to analyze customer feedback for the skincare line and research potential projects for the production company. AI handles data analysis and initial research, then the team adds strategic insights and relationship building. "AI does the heavy lifting on research and analysis, then my team focuses on the creative and relationship aspects that actually close deals."

Family Logistics Coordinator: Her part-time nanny uses AI to plan meals based on dietary needs, coordinate kids' activities with Aria's travel schedule, and manage household operations. "AI helps plan and organize, but my nanny adds the personal touch and flexibility that kids actually need."

Content and Marketing Strategist: Aria's assistant uses AI to create content frameworks and analyze market trends, but Aria adds the personal stories and authentic voice that create real connection. "We use AI for research and structure, then I make it authentically mine. It's like having a research team and creative team all in one."

Aria is scaling multiple businesses while being present for her children's childhood. She's not working more hours or spending more money, she's working smarter with a small team that leverages AI to accomplish what used to require much larger teams.

"The secret isn't money or massive teams, it's smart systems," Aria explains. "AI allows a small, strategic team to operate like a much larger organization. You just have to be willing to think bigger about what's possible when humans and AI work together."

How I Built My AI Support Team

Client Presentations That Actually Engage: AI helps me create presentations and trainings that keep people awake (amazing concept, I know). I give it my topic, bullet and audience, and it suggests ways to make boring concepts interesting. No more death by PowerPoint, just content that people remember and use.

Personal Styling Without the Price Tag: This one was a total game changer for my wardrobe confidence. I take photos of outfits I love, and AI finds similar affordable pieces. It even suggests combinations from clothes I already own but never thought of putting together. No more closet paralysis when I have a big meeting.

Publicist's Secret Weapon: My publicist uses AI to brainstorm pitch ideas and research opportunities faster than ever. She feeds it event details and trending topics, and it helps craft angles that make me stand out. What used to take hours of research now happens in minutes.

Gift Giving That Actually Impresses: AI has become my secret weapon for not being the person who gives generic candles to everyone. I describe someone's personality and interests, and it suggests gifts that make people think I pay attention to their lives (which I do, but now I have help remembering the details).

Relationship Tracking That Isn't Creepy: After conversations or events, I make quick notes in my AI system: "Caught up with Sandra - she's stressed about her mom's health" or "Linda's son just made varsity." Weeks later, through tasks that I set up, AI helps me follow up thoughtfully: "You mentioned Sandra was dealing with her mom's health issues last month. Here's a caring check-in message that acknowledges that stress." It's like having a relationship assistant who helps me be the friend I want to be, not the one who forgets everything the moment we hang up.

The best part? I can focus on the creative stuff and building real relationships while AI handles all the details that used to make my brain hurt.

Meet Your New Butler, Maid, Publicist, and Personal Assistant—All in One App

I'M JUGGLING 50 THINGS AND DROPPING EVERYTHING

AI IS MY INVISIBLE TEAM HANDLING EVERYTHING SMOOTHLY

💭 TAKE A PAUSE, FRIEND

Before we dive into building your own AI support team, take a moment to envision what your life could look like:

1. If you had a personal assistant available 24/7, what would you want them to handle first? Schedule coordination, communication management, research, meal planning, or something else?
2. What daily tasks drain your energy most but don't require your unique skills, creativity, or personal touch?
3. How would your typical day change if all the logistics were handled smoothly and you could focus on the work and relationships that matter most?
4. Which area of your life feels most chaotic and would benefit from celebrity level coordination and support?
5. If someone else could handle all the behind the scenes work in your life, what would you spend your time creating, building, or experiencing instead?

Your answers will help you identify where to start building your AI support team for maximum impact on your daily peace and effectiveness.

How Celebrities Really Get Things Done (And You Can Too)

Here's what I want you to understand: Most successful people don't try to do everything themselves. They build teams, systems, and support that amplify their unique talents while handling everything else efficiently.

The difference isn't that they're more capable than you, it's that they've learned to focus their energy on what only they can do while delegating or systematizing everything else.

With AI, you now have access to that same level of support. You can have:

- Schedule coordination like you have a personal assistant.
- Meal planning like you have a private chef.
- Communication management like you have a publicist.
- Research and strategy like you have a business consultant.
- Wellness support like you have a personal trainer and life coach.

Here's the beautiful part: your AI support team is more reliable than celebrity staff. AI never calls in sick, never has personal drama, and never judges you for the bad decisions that you make. Plus, it works at 3 AM without overtime pay.

Building Your AI Dream Team

Think of AI as different team members for different areas of your life. Here's how to assign AI "roles":

AI as Your Executive Assistant: Schedule coordination and calendar management, email filtering and routine response handling, appointment scheduling and reminder management, travel planning and itinerary coordination, task prioritization and deadline tracking.

AI as Your Household Manager: Meal planning and grocery coordination, family schedule coordination and logistics, home maintenance reminders and vendor coordination, seasonal preparation and holiday planning, budget tracking and expense management.

AI as Your Business Strategist: Market research and competitive analysis, content planning and communication strategies, client relationship management and follow-up, project coordination and deadline management, professional development and networking support.

AI as Your Wellness Coach: Energy management and schedule optimization, self-care reminders and activity suggestions, health pattern tracking and wellness insights, stress management and emotional support, goal setting and progress celebration.

DO THIS NOW, NOT LATER

Ready to build your AI celebrity support team? Choose one experiment to start this week:

Option 1: The "I'm Drowning in My Own Success" Solution If your business or career is growing but you feel like you're barely keeping up, this one's for you. Use AI to handle one aspect of your professional life that's eating up time you'd rather spend on strategy or actual revenue-generating activities. Think research, content planning, or client follow-up, anything that's important but doesn't need your personal genius touch.

Option 2: The "My Brain Is Too Full" Experiment Pick that mental load that haunts you at 3 AM. You know—those thoughts that pop up when you're half-asleep on the way to the bathroom, and you promise yourself you'll remember in the morning (but never do). The "Oh crap, mom's birthday gift!" at midnight. The "Did I schedule the dog's vet appointment?" at 2 AM. The "What was that important thing the teacher mentioned?" while you're trying to fall back asleep.

Let AI become your external brain for capturing and organizing these mental fragments. Instead of losing sleep or forgetting (again), you'll have one place where all those random but crucial details live—and AI helps you act on them before they become emergencies.

Option 3: The "Self-Care That Actually Happens" Strategy Choose that one self-care promise you keep breaking to yourself. You know—the morning workout that becomes "tomorrow for sure," the therapy appointment you keep rescheduling, the lunch break that turns into eating at your desk again, or the bedtime routine that gets hijacked by "one more email." Ask AI to help you protect this one thing like it's a million-dollar client meeting. Because here's what we forget: You ARE the million-dollar asset that makes everything else possible.

Here's the truth: You don't need to become an AI expert overnight. You just need to stop accepting that self-abandonment is the price of success. Start with protecting just one thing that refuels you. Start small, start somewhere, but definitely start this week.

Because honestly? Your sanity is worth more than your overbooked schedule.

Advanced Celebrity-Level Strategies

Building Your Own Empire Infrastructure: For women scaling businesses or building personal brands, AI becomes your strategic planning partner. While social media management platforms handle your posting schedule, AI helps with the deeper work: analyzing your competition to spot market gaps, generating content ideas based on your expertise, drafting email sequences that sound like you (after you train it on your voice), and creating frameworks for the courses or products you've been meaning to launch. It's like having a strategic advisor who helps you work ON your business, not just IN it.

Managing Your Multi-Layered Life: When you're juggling multiple children, activities, aging parents, and your own ambitions, AI helps you create systems that keep everyone's needs visible. You input each family member's schedules, preferences, and requirements, then AI helps you spot conflicts before they happen, suggests ways to batch similar activities (like putting both kids' sports on the same side of town), creates template responses for the endless school/activity communications, and reminds you of important details you'd otherwise forget in the chaos. It's not managing your family for you—it's helping you see the full picture so you can make decisions that work for everyone instead of constantly putting out fires.

Strategic Career Investment: Instead of hoping your career will advance on its own, AI helps you strategically plan your professional growth. When you share your career goals, AI can research which skills are trending in your industry, suggest relevant online courses or certifications, help you identify thought leaders to follow and learn from, and assist in creating content that showcases your expertise. It won't network for you, but it can help you craft thoughtful LinkedIn messages, prepare talking points for industry events, and analyze job descriptions to understand what skills the market values. Think of it as your career research assistant who helps you make informed decisions about where to invest your development time.

The Lifestyle Design Advantage: This is where AI becomes your personal pattern spotter. By tracking what you tell it about your energy levels and daily outcomes, AI helps you notice trends: maybe you're most creative after morning walks, or afternoon meetings drain you more than morning ones. It can help you reflect on decisions by asking clarifying questions about your values, suggest schedule arrangements based on your stated priorities, and remind you of your bigger goals when you're caught in daily urgency. It's not designing your life for you—it's helping you see patterns and possibilities so you can design a life that actually fits who you are.

CHAPTER 11 QUICK REFERENCE

Key Mindset Shift: Success comes from building smart support systems, not doing everything yourself

Core Truth: You don't need a celebrity budget to access celebrity-level organization—you need to use AI strategically

Action Step: Choose one area of overwhelm and implement AI support this week

Remember: The most successful women aren't juggling more—they're leveraging better

> " You were never meant to be a one-woman show. Even the biggest celebrities have teams—yours just happens to be digital.
>
> —T. RENEÉ SMITH "

PART III

THE MULTI-ROLE WOMAN: LEADING IN LOVE, FAMILY, BUSINESS & LIFE

> *"You're not just one thing. You're a wife, mother, daughter, professional, friend—and AI helps you show up fully in each role without losing yourself in the process."*
>
> – T. Reneé Smith

The Day I Realized I Was Playing Everyone But Myself

It was during a particularly chaotic week when I had back-to-back client calls, my bonus daughter needed advice about a situation she was navigating, one of my sons was having friend challenges, my mom called about her doctor's appointment, and my husband was dealing with work stress. I found myself switching between roles so quickly I was getting whiplash: CEO T.

Reneé to Problem-Solving Mom T. Reneé to Caring Daughter T. Reneé to Understanding Wife T. Reneé.

By the end of the week, I was sitting in my car after a client meeting, staring at my phone with seventeen different people needing their own version of me, and I had this startling realization: I was doing a really good job playing all these roles, but I had completely lost track of who I actually was underneath all of them.

Sound familiar?

The better you get at showing up for everyone else, the easier it becomes to lose yourself in the process. You become so good at being what everyone needs that you forget you're allowed to have needs too.

You know what I'm talking about. At work, you're the strategic leader who has all the answers. With your kids, you're the nurturing mother who solves all the problems. With your partner, you're the supportive wife who makes everything easier. With your aging parents, you're the capable daughter who handles all the logistics. With your friends, you're the reliable one who's always available to listen.

And somewhere in the middle of being everything to everyone, you start to wonder: Who am I when I'm not performing a role for someone else?

The Role-Playing Trap We All Fall Into

Most successful high-achieving woman struggle with the exhausting pressure to be perfect in every single role you play.

We've been conditioned to believe that being a "good" woman means excelling at everything simultaneously. You should be a rockstar professional AND a present mother AND a supportive wife AND a caring daughter AND a loyal friend AND somehow maintain your own identity and goals in whatever time is left over (spoiler alert: there isn't any).

But here's what happens when you try to be perfect in every role: You end up giving everyone else your best energy while running on fumes yourself. You become so focused on meeting everyone else's expectations that you lose touch with your own needs, desires, and dreams.

The truth is you can't be everything to everyone all the time. And trying to do so isn't just exhausting, it's impossible. Different roles require different energy, different skills, and sometimes different versions of yourself.

This is where AI becomes incredibly valuable: It helps you navigate the complexity of your multiple roles without losing yourself in the process. It supports you in being intentional about when to show up in which role, how to transition between them gracefully, and most importantly, how to maintain your own identity while serving others.

What This Section Will Do for Your Life

In Part II, we explored how AI supports every dimension of who you are—your soul, body, heart, mind, and environment. Now we're diving into the practical ways AI helps you excel in the specific roles you lead in every day.

Here's what we're covering:

Chapter 12: She Leads as a Wife & Partner - Using AI to navigate the dance between masculine and feminine energy, strengthen communication, and create deeper intimacy in your marriage

Chapter 13: She Leads as a Mom - How AI helps you parent with intention instead of survival mode, whether you're raising strong-willed children, managing blended families, or supporting neurodivergent kids

Chapter 14: She Leads as a Daughter & Caregiver - Getting AI support for the sandwich generation challenges, aging parent care, and maintaining your own well-being while caring for others

Chapter 15: She Leads as a Professional - How to become irreplaceable in your career by combining AI efficiency with distinctly human brilliance

Chapter 16: She Leads as a CEO & Business Owner - The blueprint for building a business using AI that scales efficiently without requiring you to scale your stress

Each chapter shows you how AI amplifies your natural leadership abilities in each role—without trying to make you someone you're not.

The Integration, Not Balance, Approach

I believe balance is a myth that's been making us crazy for decades.

Balance implies that all your roles should get equal time and energy, which is not only impossible but also unnecessary. Some seasons of life require more focus on your career or business. Others require more attention to family. Some days your aging parents need you more. Other days your business needs you more.

Instead of balance, what we're really seeking is integration—the ability to flow between your different roles with intention and grace, giving each role what it needs when it needs it, without sacrificing your core identity.

AI helps with integration by:

- Helping you identify what each role needs from you (versus what you think it needs)
- Supporting you in setting appropriate boundaries so one role doesn't consume all your energy
- Providing strategies for transitioning between roles mindfully
- Reminding you that you're not required to be perfect in every role simultaneously
- Helping you maintain your own identity and goals while serving others

In the chapters that follow, we're going to explore how AI can support you in each of the major roles you play: as a mother, as a wife and partner, as a daughter and caregiver, as a professional or as a business owner. But more importantly, we're going to talk about how to use AI to ensure that while you're busy taking care of everyone else, you don't lose yourself in the process.

Because here's what I've learned: The most powerful thing you can do for everyone you love is to remain connected to who you are underneath all the roles you play. When you're grounded in your own identity, values, and needs, you can show up more authentically and sustainably in every role.

You're not just a collection of roles and responsibilities. You're a whole person with your own dreams, goals, and desires. And you deserve support in honoring all of who you are, not just the parts that serve other people.

Let's explore how AI can help you master the art of role integration while keeping yourself at the center of your own life.

CHAPTER 12

SHE LEADS AS A WIFE & PARTNER: DANCING BETWEEN BOSS AND BELOVED

> *"The strongest women know when to lead with strategy and when to lead with softness—and that both are forms of power."*
> – T. Reneé Smith

The Conversation Where I Almost Chose My Ego Over My Marriage

Have you ever had one of those conversations with your husband where deep down you knew he was right, but you were going to get defensive anyway just to save face?

Picture this: My husband is trying to share something important with me, and instead of listening, I'm sitting there mentally preparing my rebuttal. I can't wait for him to finish talking so I can launch into my perfectly crafted list of bullet points about why he's wrong. So naturally, I interrupt him mid-sentence.

And that, as you can imagine, was about as effective as trying to put out a fire with gasoline.

"Can you just let me finish?" he said, with that particular tone that means you've really stepped over the line this time.

But did I apologize and listen? Of course not. I doubled down with something brilliant like, "I was just trying to set the record straight about what I actually said," which is wife-speak for "I'd rather be right than happy, and I'm about to prove it with receipts."

What followed was one of those conversations that could have either brought us closer together or sent us to opposite corners of the house for the rest of the evening. Thankfully, something in his voice made me realize I was about to choose my ego over my marriage, and that was not a trade I was willing to make.

Here's what he was trying to tell me: "You know how you are with the kids? All soft and nurturing and intuitive? I miss that version of you sometimes. It's like you come home in full CEO mode, ready to strategize and solve problems and optimize everything. But sometimes I just want to experience the softer, more feminine side of you, the one that shows up so naturally with our children."

And here's the part that made me want to crawl under a rock: He was right. I could shift into nurturing mama mode with my kids without even thinking about it, but with him, I was treating every conversation like a board meeting where I needed to defend my position and win the argument.

That conversation taught me that I didn't need to choose between my masculine and feminine energy, I needed to learn when to use each one. And honestly, learning to tap into my feminine energy in my marriage was harder than any business strategy I'd ever mastered.

The High-Achieving Woman's Energy Evolution

Can we talk about something that affects many successful women but rarely gets discussed honestly? Most of us have been operating in masculine energy for so long—both at work and at home—that we've forgotten the power of integrating both energies in all areas of our lives.

Here's what typically happens: You've built your success on masculine energy—being decisive, strategic, goal-oriented, making things happen. And it works. You get promoted, close deals, lead teams, build businesses. So naturally, you double down on what's working.

But here's what we miss: The most magnetic and effective leaders know how to dance between both energies at work and at home. They use masculine energy for strategic planning and feminine energy for intuitive decision-making. They lead with authority when setting direction and with receptivity when building team culture. They problem-solve with logic and create with flow.

The challenge is that many of us are stuck in "prove it" mode. We're so focused on demonstrating our competence that we've abandoned half of our power. We think showing feminine energy at work means being weak, when it's what separates good leaders from extraordinary ones.

Think about it: Your best negotiations happen when you combine strategic thinking (masculine) with reading the room (feminine). Your most innovative solutions come from structured analysis (masculine) meeting creative intuition (feminine). Your strongest teams form when you balance clear expectations (masculine) with emotional intelligence (feminine).

But instead, we operate like this: Masculine energy all day at work. Try to switch to feminine at home. Fail because we're exhausted and out of practice. Oftentimes we bring that same all-masculine energy to our marriages. Wondering why we feel disconnected from ourselves AND our partners.

Let me be crystal clear: Feminine energy isn't weakness. It's not being passive or submissive or losing yourself. Feminine energy is intuition, creativity, receptivity, flow, nurturing, and the ability to create space for others to show up fully. It's a different kind of strength—one that makes you MORE powerful at work, not less.

The real challenge for ambitious women isn't learning to switch between energies when we get home. It's learning to integrate both energies throughout our entire day, so we're not exhausted from being half of ourselves for 8-10 hours straight.

Meet Victoria: When the Breadwinner Has to Learn to Be the Bride

Victoria, a 55-year-old Fortune 500 Executive Vice-President, got married for the first time just ten months ago. Victoria wasn't just successful, she was the breadwinner, making significantly more than her husband, a confident man who owned a small consulting firm.

"I thought being the financial provider would be the hard part of our relationship," Victoria laughed. "Turns out, the real challenge was learning that 'wife' and 'life coach' are two different job descriptions, and I'd somehow appointed myself to the second position without his consent."

Here's what Victoria discovered: When you're used to being the one who pays the bills, makes the big decisions, and solves all the problems, it's incredibly difficult to step back and let your partner lead in other areas. She had taken on all the traditionally masculine roles, providing, protecting, and decision-making, and had forgotten how to access her feminine energy.

"My husband is this wonderfully confident man who knew exactly what he was getting into when he married a high-powered executive," Victoria explained. "But he also knew that for our marriage to work, I was going to have to learn how to be a wife, not just a leader who happened to live in his house."

The power struggle was real. Victoria was used to having the final say because, well, she was paying for everything. Her husband was used to being respected as a man and partner, regardless of who made more money. Something had to give.

"The breaking point came when I tried to 'manage' his response to a work situation," Victoria admitted. "I literally said, 'Here's how you should handle that,' and he looked at me and said, 'Victoria, I'm your husband, not your employee. You can't promote me or fire me, and you definitely can't micromanage me.'"

Ouch. But also, completely fair.

Victoria realized she had become so good at leading in masculine energy: strategic, decisive, protective, providing, that she had forgotten how to flow in feminine energy: receptive, trusting, supportive, nurturing. And her marriage was suffocating under the weight of her need to control everything.

"I was terrified of being vulnerable," Victoria confessed. "When you're the breadwinner, you feel like you have to be strong all the time. But my husband didn't need me to be strong for him, he needed me to be soft with him."

Here's how AI helped Victoria navigate the complex dynamics of being a high-earning wife:

Power Dynamic Awareness: Victoria would describe situations to AI where she felt compelled to take charge: "My husband mentioned wanting to invest in new equipment for his consulting firm, and I immediately started analyzing his ROI projections." AI would respond with clarifying questions: "What would happen if you trusted his business judgment here? What are you afraid might occur if you're not directing this decision?"

Through these daily check-ins, Victoria began recognizing her control patterns. AI helped her see that her need to lead everything came from fear—fear that if she wasn't in charge, things would fall apart. This awareness helped her ask herself before jumping in: "Am I trying to control this because it truly needs my input, or because I'm uncomfortable not being the decision-maker?

Feminine Energy Practice: Victoria told AI: "I walk in the door and immediately start managing everything—dinner plans, household decisions, even how my husband should handle his work stress." AI suggested unexpected ways to access her feminine energy:

"What brings you joy without any productive outcome? When do you feel most creative and flowing?" Victoria realized she used to love dancing but hadn't danced in years—too "frivolous" for a Fortune 500 executive. AI encouraged her: "Put on music while cooking dinner. Move your body without choreography. Let your husband see you enjoying something just for the joy of it."

AI also suggested sensory practices: "Change into soft fabrics when you get home. Light candles. Engage your senses rather than your strategy." When Victoria slipped into fix-it mode during conversations, AI had taught her to pause and ask herself: "Is he inviting me to feel with him or fix for him?" This simple question changed how she responded to her husband's shares.

Trust Building: When Victoria caught herself micromanaging, she'd tell AI what happened. AI would guide her through the fear: "You just rewrote your husband's client proposal. What did you worry would happen if you didn't?" Victoria would realize she feared his business failing and reflecting poorly on her. AI helped her reframe: "His business success or challenges are his journey. Your role is support, not prevention of all possible failures." AI provided specific phrases: "When you want to take over, try I'm here if you want to brainstorm" instead of "Let me handle this."

Financial Boundary Setting: Victoria asked AI: "How do I handle money decisions when I make 3x what my husband does?" AI helped her create categories: "List what financial decisions genuinely need your input (joint investments, major purchases) versus what you're controlling just because you can (his business expenses, his personal purchases)." AI then helped her practice conversations: Instead of "I don't think you should buy that," try "What's your thinking on this purchase?" Show curiosity about his decision-making rather than oversight.

Vulnerability Coaching: Victoria struggled with letting her guard down. She'd tell AI: "I feel weak when I'm not in control." AI would explore this: "What does 'weak' mean to you? What might your husband experience when you're always strong?" AI helped her practice vulnerable statements: "I'm scared that if I'm not managing everything, something bad will happen" instead of maintaining her everything's-fine facade. AI also suggested couple's exercises: "Share one area where you'd like his leadership this week."

Victoria's marriage went from feeling like a business partnership where she was the senior partner to feeling like an actual partnership where both people contributed different strengths.

"The hardest thing I had to learn was that my husband didn't need me to take care of him financially, emotionally, and mentally," Victoria explains. "He needed me to trust him enough to take care of his areas of expertise while I focused on taking care of mine. And honestly, it was the most freeing thing I'd ever experienced."

"AI helped me realize that being the breadwinner doesn't mean being the bread-everything-er," Victoria laughs. "I could contribute financially and still receive emotionally. I could lead at work and follow at home. I could be strong in my career and soft in my marriage. Turns out, I didn't have to choose, I just had to learn when to access which energy."

Meet Sofia: When Your Marriage Gets Your Leftovers

Sofia is a 42-year-old corporate lawyer who calls herself "a recovering workaholic with intimacy issues." Sofia and her husband are both ambitious professionals, but they were struggling with what she calls "the classic high-achiever marriage trap."

"We were both giving our best energy to our careers and our leftover, exhausted energy to each other," Sofia explained. "I could be sharp and focused in court for eight hours, charming with difficult clients, and patient with demanding partners at my firm. But by the time I got home, I was basically a shell of myself with nothing left for meaningful conversation, much less marriage ministry."

(Yes, she borrowed my term for intimacy, and I'm absolutely here for it.)

But here's what really got to her: Let a client call during dinner, and suddenly Sofia would transform like Clark Kent finding a phone booth. She'd perk up, become fully engaged, and give that person her complete attention—meanwhile her husband's watching her wondering if he needs to start billing her for his time just to get on her calendar.

"I realized I was more patient, more attentive, and more emotionally available for my work relationships than for my own husband," she admitted. "That was a hard pill to swallow."

Sofia had fallen into the trap so many successful women face unconsciously treating her marriage like it could run on autopilot while she poured everything into her career. She was showing up as her absolute best self for clients, colleagues, and court cases, but giving her husband whatever crumbs of energy remained at the end of the day.

"The worst part was that I wouldn't dream of treating a client the way I was treating my husband. I'd never give a client half my attention or respond to their concerns with can we talk about this later, I'm exhausted."

Here's how AI helped Sofia flip the script:

Energy Tracking: Sofia told AI about her typical day: "I was charming with a difficult client for two hours, then came home and snapped at my husband for leaving dishes in the sink." AI helped her track patterns: "Let's log your energy levels throughout the day. Rate yourself 1-10 after each major interaction." After a week, the data was brutal: 9s and 10s for client meetings, 2s and 3s for evening conversations with her husband. AI made it visual: "You're giving premium energy to people who pay you and exhausted energy to the person who loves you. How does seeing this pattern make you feel?"

Boundary Creation: When Sofia said, "I can't ignore client calls during dinner," AI challenged her: "You don't take calls during court proceedings. Why is your marriage less worthy of protected time?" AI helped her create specific protocols: "Let's draft an after-hours auto-response that sets expectations. Now, what ritual will remind you to power down?" Sofia chose to plug her phone in the kitchen at 7 PM—physically removing the temptation. AI checked in daily: "Did you honor your phone boundary tonight? What was different about your evening?"

Presence Practice: Sofia complained to AI: "I can't switch off lawyer brain." AI suggested experimenting: "Before entering your house, name five things you're grateful for about your husband—out loud, in your car. It's hard to stay in lawyer mode when you're actively appreciating your partner." AI also provided conversation starters that bypassed work talk: "Instead of 'How was your day' try 'What made you laugh today?' or 'What are you looking forward to this week?'"

Relationship Planning: Sofia told AI, "We haven't had sex in three weeks, and I'm too exhausted to care." AI responded: "You prepare for major cases weeks in advance. What if you applied 1% of that planning to your intimate life?" AI helped her recognize patterns: "You have the most energy on Thursday evenings. What if you protected Thursdays for connection?" It wasn't about scheduling sex but about creating conditions where connection could naturally happen—like planning date nights with the same care she planned client dinners.

Within months, Sofia's marriage felt completely different. She was finally showing up as her best self for her husband instead of her burnt-out, leftover self, and their connection deepened in ways that surprised them both.

"AI helped me realize that my marriage deserved the same level of care and attention I was giving to my career," Sofia explains. "Once I started treating my relationship like it actually mattered as much as my work, everything shifted."

How I Use AI for Marriage Energy Management

Let me share how AI helps me navigate the daily dance between being a CEO and being a wife:

The Outcome Check-In: Before I engage in a heated discussion with my husband, AI helps me pause and ask myself: "Do I want to be right, or do I want to be happy? What outcome am I looking for in my interactions, and is my current energy going to get me there?" This simple question completely changes how I show up for my husband.

The Deposit vs. Withdrawal Assessment: AI helped me create a simple check-in ritual where I ask myself: "Am I showing up as my full self, ready to serve and make a deposit into my husband, or am I looking to make a withdrawal from an account that's already empty?" This one question shifted how I approach our time together.

The Listening Practice: When my husband is sharing something with me, AI reminds me to ask myself: "Does he need me to solve this, or does he need me to hear this?" Nine times out of ten, he just needs me to listen and be present.

The Energy Protection: AI helps me set work hour boundaries that protect energy for my marriage. This means no working after I leave to pick up my youngest son (unless something's literally on fire and no one else has a fire hose), not bringing work stress into our bedroom, and treating our relationship time as sacred and non-negotiable.

Mastering Your Masculine-Feminine Flow

Most ambitious women are operating with only half their power because they don't realize this: the difference between masculine and feminine energy and why both are essential for thriving in all areas of your life.

First, let me be crystal clear: This has nothing to do with gender stereotypes or traditional roles. This is about energy and approach, and every person has access to both.

Masculine Energy: This is your strategic, analytical, goal-oriented, decisive, problem-solving energy. It's focused, directional, and action oriented. It creates structure, safety, results, and forward movement. You need this energy for leading teams, making tough decisions, and driving projects forward.

Feminine Energy: This is your intuitive, receptive, flowing, nurturing energy. It's present, creative, and connection oriented. It creates space, warmth, collaboration, and emotional intimacy. You need this energy for inspired action, creative solutions, and building meaningful relationships.

The wisest women know how to access both energies and use them appropriately in every area of their lives. At work, you might need masculine energy for strategic planning and feminine energy for creative brainstorming. At home, you might need masculine energy for organizing schedules and meal planning, and feminine energy for intimate conversations with your partner. The key is consciousness and choice about which energy serves each situation best, not defaulting to one mode all the time.

Being fully aligned means assessing what each moment requires and showing up accordingly, whether that's at the boardroom table or the dinner table.

Here's what happens when we get stuck in only one energy mode in our marriages:

- Every conversation becomes either a strategy session or an emotional processing session
- We either solve everything or avoid all practical decisions
- We either compete with our partner or become completely passive
- We either optimize everything or refuse to plan anything
- We either manage every detail or let everything fall apart

But here's what happens when we learn to dance between both energies:

- We can be strategic when planning and intuitive when connecting
- We can lead when direction is needed and flow when presence is required
- We can solve problems efficiently and create emotional intimacy naturally
- We can be successful in our goals and deeply connected in our relationships
- We can bring structure when needed and create space for spontaneity

AI helps with this balance by:

- Helping you recognize which energy each situation needs, whether it's organizing the family calendar or having an intimate conversation

- Providing transition practices that help you shift between energies throughout your day

- Reminding you that both energies are valuable and necessary in all areas of life

- Supporting you in accessing the full range of your capabilities instead of defaulting to one mode

- Helping you communicate your needs and understand your partner's needs in each moment

She Leads as a Wife & Partner

💭 TAKE A PAUSE, FRIEND

Before we dive into practical applications, pour yourself some tea and honestly reflect on these questions:

1. When you come home from work, what energy do you bring to your marriage? Are you still in strategic mode, or do you intentionally transition into relationship mode?
2. How do you typically respond when your partner shares problems with you? Do you immediately jump to solutions, or do you listen and provide emotional support first?
3. When do you feel most connected to your partner? Think about whether those moments happen when you're both focused on tasks and goals, or when you're focused on each other and just being together.
4. What would change in your relationship if you brought the same intentionality to your marriage that you bring to your most important work projects?
5. How easy is it for you to switch between being the one who takes charge and the one who goes with the flow? What beliefs do you have about when each approach is right?

Your answers will help you identify where you might need to rebalance your energy and approach to create the marriage you truly desire.

Beyond Management: AI for Marriage Ministry

While managing the logistics of shared life is important, AI's real power lies in helping ambitious women access the deeper emotional intelligence needed for true intimacy—something many of us have buried under years of professional armor.

Feeling Recognition: AI helps you identify what you're feeling beyond "fine" or "tired" by asking questions like "What's underneath your frustration right now?" and helps you share those real emotions with your partner instead of defaulting to surface-level updates.

Vulnerability Coaching: AI coaches you through sharing your real emotional state with phrases like "I'm struggling today and could use some emotional support" instead of defaulting to "I've got it all handled" when you're barely keeping it together.

Joy Rediscovery: AI asks you questions that help you remember what brings you joy beyond productivity: "When did you last feel truly playful with your partner?" and suggests ways to invite more of those moments into your marriage.

Receiving Practice: AI coaches you through accepting compliments, help, and affection without immediately deflecting ("Thank you" instead of "This old thing?") or reciprocating ("Let me just enjoy this" instead of "Now what can I do for you?").

> **Pleasure Prioritizing:** AI reminds you that intimacy deserves the same planning and attention you give to important meetings. Because let's be honest—hoping for spontaneous passion after a long day usually ends with you fake-snoring when your husband scoots closer, praying he'll think you're too deep in REM sleep to notice. AI helps you prepare mentally and emotionally for connection when you have energy for it.
>
> **Surrender Support:** AI guides you through the uncomfortable but necessary practice of stepping back when your partner wants to handle something, coaching you with phrases like "I trust you with this" when every instinct tells you to take control.

DO THIS NOW, NOT LATER

Ready to use AI to show up more presently in your marriage? Choose one experiment to try this week:

Option 1: The Energy Audit Flip For one week, ask your husband to rate your energy when you come home (1-10, with 10 being fully present and connected). Don't tell him why—just ask for the number. Then ask AI: "My husband rated my energy as a [number] today. Based on common relationship dynamics, what behaviors might contribute to this rating? What specific actions could help me show up more present and connected tomorrow?" Use AI to help you identify patterns and practical changes rather than guessing what's working or not.

Option 2: The Feminine Energy Challenge Choose one traditionally "masculine" household task you always handle (finances, home repairs, strategic planning). Ask AI: "How can I approach [task] from feminine energy—intuitive, collaborative, flowing—and invite my husband to lead?" Try this role reversal for one week and notice what shifts in your dynamic.

Option 3: The Play Practice Ask AI: "Help me brainstorm 10 ways to be playful with my husband that have nothing to do with productivity or goals." Pick one each day—maybe it's a random dance party while cooking, a silly voice message during his workday, or hiding flirty notes where he'll find them. Track how play changes your connection.

Option 4: The Curiosity Experiment For one week, approach your husband like you're meeting him for the first time. Ask AI: "Give me 7 questions to ask my husband that we've never discussed in [number] years of marriage." Use one per day. Examples: "What's a dream you've never told me about?" "What memory from childhood still makes you smile?" Watch how curiosity revives connection.

Choose the option that feels most relevant to your current relationship dynamics and commit to trying it consistently for one week.

> **CHAPTER 12 QUICK REFERENCE**
>
> **Key Mindset Shift**: Your marriage thrives when you can be both the strategic woman who leads and the receptive woman who loves, and knowing when each is needed
>
> **Core Truth**: Your husband deserves the best of you, not whatever's left after you've given everything to everyone else
>
> **Action Step**: Choose one AI relationship experiment to try consistently for one week
>
> **Remember**: You don't have to choose between being powerful and being soft, you can be both, and your marriage needs both

> " The most magnetic women don't choose between masculine and feminine energy—they master the dance between both, at work and at home.
>
> — T. Reneé Smith "

CHAPTER 13

SHE LEADS AS A MOM: RAISING TINY HUMANS WHO THINK THEY RUN THE WORLD

> "The children who challenge you the most today are often the ones who will change the world tomorrow."
> – T. Reneé Smith

The Prayer That Backfired Spectacularly

I want to share the prayer that changed my entire perspective on motherhood, and not in the way I expected.

For years, I prayed for strong-willed children. I wanted to raise kids who were critical thinkers, natural leaders, able to handle pressure with grace, resilient in the face of challenges, and empathetic to others. I dreamed of children who would stand up for what's right, voice their opinions confidently, and lead with integrity instead of just following the crowd.

God apparently has a sense of humor, because He gave me exactly what I asked for.

I thought "strong-willed" meant they'd be independent thinkers who happened to still listen to me. What I got were tiny humans who questioned everything I said, negotiated every request like they were closing a business deal, and somehow turned "clean your room" into a 45-minute philosophical debate about personal freedom and property rights.

One morning, I found myself in a "discussion" with my youngest son about his outfit choice, three completely different shades of red from his shirt, shorts, and shoes. He felt confident in his look and couldn't understand why I wanted him to change into something that matched. (His position: he loved how he looked and didn't care what anyone else thought. My position: people are going to notice, sweetie.) Ten minutes later, I realized that my son had won that battle, and here's the kicker, I can negotiate million-dollar client deals all day long, but apparently my superpowers don't work on my own child.

That's when I had my revelation: I wasn't raising compliant children who would make my life easier. I was raising future leaders who happened to be practicing their leadership skills on me first. And honestly, I needed a better strategy than "because I said so" and hoping for the best.

The Strong-Willed Child Reality Check

Here's the truth about what it's really like to parent children with opinions. Because the parenting books make it sound like strong-willed kids are just "spirited" and need "gentle guidance."

What they don't tell you is that strong-willed children are basically tiny entrepreneurs who see every household rule as a hostile takeover attempt. They don't throw tantrums, they hold board meetings where they present detailed arguments about why bedtime is unconstitutional and vegetables are a violation of their human rights.

My kids can spot inconsistency from three rooms away. If I say, "maybe later" and mean "absolutely not," they file that information away and bring it up six months later during completely unrelated negotiations. They remember every exception I've ever made and use it as legal precedent for why the current rule doesn't apply.

But here's what I've learned: independent thinking children aren't trying to make your life difficult (okay, sometimes they are, but mostly they're not). They're trying to understand the world, test boundaries, and figure out how things work. The problem is most of us parents are trying to manage them instead of leading them.

This is where AI became my secret weapon for channeling their leadership energy productively.

Meet Amanda: Blending Families Without Losing Your Sanity

Amanda, a 36-year-old nurse, thought she understood children until she became a stepmother to three kids while also having two of her own.

"I was basically running a small United Nations," Amanda laughed. "Five kids between ages 5 and 14, two different parenting styles, and approximately seventeen different opinions on everything from what constitutes breakfast to whether homework is cruel and unusual punishment."

Amanda's biggest challenge wasn't the logistics, it was the family politics. Her step kids had perfected the art of playing parents against each other, her biological kids were convinced she loved them less because she was "being nice" to the new kids, and every family decision became a negotiation between multiple parties with competing interests.

"The worst part was feeling like I was failing everyone," Amanda told me. I'd be strict with my stepson about screen time, and he'd say, "dad doesn't make me do this." Then I'd be lenient with my daughter, and she'd wonder why her stepbrother got different treatment. I felt like a terrible mother and an even worse stepmother.

Here's how AI helped Amanda create actual harmony in her blended family chaos:

The Individual Kid Strategy: Amanda described each child's typical reactions to AI: "My 14-year-old stepdaughter rolls her eyes and says whatever to every request. My 7-year-old melts down when he doesn't understand why he has to do something." AI analyzed these patterns and suggested: "Your stepdaughter's response is her way of saying you're not respecting her intelligence. Try giving her choices—would you prefer to handle dishes tonight or tomorrow morning? Your 7-year-old needs the why before the what. Instead of just saying clean your room, try explaining that cleaning helps him find his favorite toys easier."

Amanda tested these approaches and saw immediate changes in cooperation.

The United Front Approach: When Amanda vented to AI about kids manipulating the parent divide, AI helped her create a response system. "My stepson just told me his dad lets him stay up until 10," Amanda typed. AI suggested: "First, don't contradict his dad in front of him. Tell him that's interesting and you'll sync with Dad about bedtime. Then text your husband immediately."

AI helped them create a shared document of house rules that both parents could reference, eliminating the guessing game.

The New Traditions Creator: Amanda asked AI: "How do I bond with five kids who have nothing in common besides living in the same house?" AI first asked her to list each child's interests and personality traits. After Amanda provided details, AI suggested: "Create expertise nights where each child becomes the teacher. Your stepdaughter who loves baking could lead monthly dessert-making sessions. Your gaming stepson could host family Minecraft building competitions. Your youngest who loves Legos could challenge everyone to weekly building contests. This positions each child as valued for their unique skills."

AI also provided conversation starters for each activity to help deeper connections form naturally during these shared experiences.

The Conflict Resolution System: They're constantly saying it's not fair that rules are different for different kids," Amanda told AI. AI helped her reframe fairness: "Ask each child what fair means to them, then guide them to see that fair means everyone gets what they need, not everyone gets the same thing."

AI provided age-appropriate scripts: For younger kids: "You need earlier bedtime because your body needs more sleep to grow strong." For older kids: "You have more freedom because you've shown you can handle responsibility. Your siblings will earn these privileges too as they grow." AI also suggested creating a privilege progression chart showing what each age could work toward, making the system transparent rather than arbitrary.

"AI helped me realize that blended families don't work when you try to force everyone into traditional family roles," Amanda explains. "They work when you create new systems that honor everyone's personality and history while building something totally new together."

Meet Linda: Single Parenting with Humor and Strategy

Linda is a 43-year-old pediatric psychologist and single mother to neurodivergent twin boys. She'll tell you that professional training in child psychology prepared her for exactly nothing when it came to parenting her own brilliant and complicated children.

"People assume that because I'm a psychologist, my kids should be perfectly behaved," Linda laughed. "But professional knowledge and 2 AM meltdowns are completely different skill sets. Plus, these kids know I'm a psychologist, so they've basically been therapy-proofing themselves since birth."

Linda's twin boys are like a psychological case study in how two children can share DNA and absolutely nothing else. One has ADHD and anxiety and needs constant movement and stimulation. The other has autism and sensory processing differences and needs routine and quiet. What helps one often overwhelms the other, and Linda felt like she was running a very specialized daycare for genius level children who happened to live in her house.

"The hardest part was feeling like I should know what to do," Linda admitted. "When other parents ask for advice, I can help them. When my own kid is having a meltdown because his socks feel 'wrong,' all my training goes out the window and I'm just a mom trying not to cry in the laundry room."

Here's how AI became Linda's strategic parenting partner:

The Pattern Detective: Linda would log daily observations into AI: "Jamie had a meltdown at 4 PM when I asked him to start homework. He threw his backpack and hid under the table." AI helped her see patterns: "You've logged similar reactions every day at 4 PM. This timing suggests he's not being defiant—he's experiencing transition overload. His ADHD brain is still processing the school day."

AI suggested: "Try a 30-minute movement break before homework. Let him jump on the trampoline or ride his bike to discharge the school energy first." For her autistic son, AI noticed: "You report Max being 'rude' to guests, but it always happens after school events. He's overstimulated and needs quiet time before social interactions.

The Social Skills Coach: When Linda asked AI for help with playground struggles, it provided specific strategies: "For Jamie's ADHD impulsivity during games, teach him the phrase—Can I have a turn next? —instead of grabbing. Practice this at home with preferred activities first." For Max's autism-related social challenges, AI suggested: "Don't force eye contact. Teach him to look at people's foreheads or ears—it appears like eye contact without the sensory overload. Also, give him conversation starter cards with questions like What's your favorite Minecraft build? This works better than expecting spontaneous small talk.

The Advocacy Assistant: Linda typed her frustrations into AI: "The school says Max doesn't qualify for support because his grades are fine." AI helped her reframe: "Stop leading with his academic performance. Focus on the energy cost of him maintaining those grades. Bring examples like: Max holds it together at school but has two-hour meltdowns at home. This shows he's working ten times harder than other kids just to keep up. Use parent impact language, not clinical terms—say my child is exhausted and miserable instead of he exhibits signs of autistic burnout.

The Sanity Saver: When Linda felt guilty about needing breaks, she'd tell AI: "I should be able to handle this. I'm trained for this." AI would remind her: "You're trained to be a psychologist for 8 hours a day with other people's children. You're parenting 24/7 with your own trauma triggers and emotional investment. Would you tell a client they should never need respite?" AI helped her find specific resources: local special needs parent groups, respite care programs her insurance covered, and even helped her practice asking friends for help without over-explaining or apologizing.

The results were beautiful. Linda's boys developed more confidence in social situations, their academic performance improved because they had better support, and Linda felt more equipped to handle daily challenges without burning out or questioning every decision.

"AI helped me organize my thoughts, stay consistent with strategies even when I was exhausted, and remember that being a good mom doesn't mean being a perfect psychologist."

How I Use AI for Real-World Motherhood

AI has been extremely helpful in navigating the daily adventure of raising strong-willed kids:

The Negotiation Prep: When my youngest son starts his bedtime resistance—not arguing but moving incredibly slowly and suddenly needing to use the bathroom while watching his table—I quickly type to AI: "My neurodivergent son is stalling bedtime with every delay tactic possible. Help me respond with patience." AI gives me responses like: "I see you're having a hard time transitioning to bedtime. Your brain is still busy with lots of thoughts. Let's do our bedtime checklist together—first take our shower, the bathroom, brush your teeth, then read a story in bed. Your brain needs sleep to process all those amazing ideas." This acknowledges his needs while maintaining routine.

The Teaching Moment Creator: My oldest son prefers learning most things on his own without input. I asked AI: "How do I guide someone who needs to discover everything himself?" AI reframed my approach: "He's not rejecting your wisdom—he's building his own. Try being a sounding board instead of an advisor. Ask 'What's your thinking on this?' and 'What factors are you weighing?' When he shares his process, you can add 'Have you considered...' as a peer would, not as a parent directing. This respects his autonomy while keeping you in the conversation.

The Screen Time Sanity Saver: I asked AI: "Is there a way to manage my son's screen time that doesn't end in daily warfare?" AI helped me flip the script: "Instead of you policing his time, make him the manager. Give him weekly screen hours and let him budget it. Want to binge Saturday? Fine, but Sunday is screen-free. He learns time management and you stop being the screen police."

The Exhausted Parent Support: You know those moments when you become the parent you swore you'd never be? Like when you hear yourself yelling "BECAUSE I SAID SO!"—the exact phrase that made you crazy as a kid? Yeah, that was me the other night.

After years of teaching my kids about emotional regulation and taking deep breaths, I completely lost it when they announced they were hungry (despite the full dinner I'd just served), needed craft supplies for tomorrow's project we didn't have, and wanted to plan the entire weekend's social calendar while I was mentally running on empty.

I slunk to my phone and typed to AI: "I just became my mother. Send help." AI responded with grace: "Welcome to the I Sound Like My Parents club. Every member swears it won't happen, then it does. Here's your recovery plan: Own it with humor. Try telling them: Kids, remember when Mom just turned into a fire-breathing dragon? That wasn't my best moment. Even grown-ups need timeouts sometimes. Who wants to help me practice my deep breathing?" AI helped me see that showing them how to recover from losing your cool is just as important as keeping it.

The "Good Mom" Myth That's Completely Wrong

Can we destroy the myth that good mothers produce perfectly behaved children? Because that's not how any of this works.

Strong-willed children aren't evidence of poor parenting; they're evidence of children who feel safe enough to express their opinions and test boundaries. Compliant children aren't necessarily well-behaved, sometimes they're just scared or haven't learned to think for themselves yet.

The goal isn't raising children who never challenge you. The goal is raising children who can think critically, advocate for themselves, and make good decisions even when you're not there to tell them what to do.

AI helps with this by:

- Teaching you to see challenging behavior as information, not defiance
- Helping you respond to your children's individual personalities instead of trying to make them fit generic molds
- Providing strategies for channeling strong-willed energy into positive leadership skills
- Supporting your confidence as a mother when your children don't match Pinterest-perfect expectations

💬 TAKE A PAUSE, FRIEND

Before we dive into practical applications, pour yourself something caffeinated (because motherhood requires all the fuel we can get) and honestly think about these questions:

1. What did you think parenting would be like versus what it's actually like? Where are the biggest gaps between expectation and reality?
2. What are your children's strongest personality traits, and how can those traits serve them well as adults (even if they're challenging now)?
3. How do you typically handle conflicts with your children? Are you managing behavior or teaching life skills?
4. What would change in your family dynamic if you felt more confident in your parenting decisions and less overwhelmed by daily power struggles?
5. If you had a parenting strategist available 24/7, what would you want them to help you with most?

Your answers will help you identify where AI can provide the most valuable support for your specific mothering challenges and goals.

Intentional Mothering: While managing the daily adventures of family life is important, AI's real power lies in helping you raise children who can think for themselves, advocate for themselves and others, and make good decisions when you're not there to guide them.

Character Development: AI helps you identify teachable moments in daily conflicts and turn them into opportunities for your children to practice integrity, empathy, and responsibility.

Individual Child Strategy: AI helps you understand each child's unique wiring and develop approaches that work with their personality instead of against it.

Long-term Vision: AI helps you balance immediate needs (like getting everyone dressed and out the door) with long-term character development (like teaching your children to consider other people's needs and make thoughtful decisions).

Crisis Preparation: AI helps you prepare for the hard conversations and situations you hope won't happen but might, peer pressure, bullying, mental health struggles, academic challenges, or safety concerns.

Legacy Building: AI helps you think beyond just raising good kids to raising children who will become adults who make the world better.

DO THIS NOW, NOT LATER

Ready to use AI for more intentional mothering? Choose one experiment to try this week:

Option 1: The Strong-Willed Child Reframe Pick your most strong-willed child and ask AI: "Help me understand how my child's [specific behavior] could be a strength when they're an adult and suggest three ways I can channel this energy positively." Try AI's suggestions for one week.

Option 2: The Teaching Moment Transformer Next time your child has a conflict, ask AI: "Help me turn this situation into a learning opportunity about [conflict resolution/empathy/problem-solving] for a child age [X]." Use AI's approach instead of just solving the problem for them.

Option 3: The Individual Child Strategy Choose one child and ask AI: "Based on this child's personality [describe them], suggest three parenting approaches that would help them develop confidence and good decision-making skills."

Implement one of AI's suggestions consistently for one week.

Choose the option that feels most relevant to your current mothering challenges and commit to trying it consistently for one week.

CHAPTER 13 QUICK REFERENCE

Key Mindset Shift: Strong-willed children aren't trying to make your life difficult, they're practicing leadership skills and need guidance, not management

Core Truth: The goal isn't raising perfect children, it's raising children who can think critically and make good decisions independently

Action Step: Choose one AI parenting experiment to try consistently for one week

Remember: You're not raising children to be convenient for you; you're raising future adults who will change the world

> The best mothers aren't the ones who raise the most compliant children, they're the ones who raise children with the courage to think for themselves and the wisdom to consider others.
>
> — T. Reneé Smith

CHAPTER 14

SHE LEADS AS A DAUGHTER & FAMILY MEMBER: THE TRUTH ABOUT BEING THE SUCCESSFUL ONE

> *"Being the successful one in the family is both a blessing and a responsibility, but you get to choose how you carry it."*
>
> – T. Reneé Smith

The Hospital Room That Made Me Chief Medical Officer (Without My Permission)

The six months my mom was in the hospital taught me more about family dynamics, sacrifice, and setting boundaries than any business school ever could.

During the day, I was running my business, leading my team, making strategic decisions, and maintaining my professional reputation. But during the evenings and on weekends, I was at the hospital learning a completely different kind of leadership, the kind that involves advocating for someone who can't advocate for themselves.

Here's what nobody prepared me for: When you're the successful one in the family, everyone automatically assumes you'll handle everything. Not just the emotional support (which I was happy to give), but the logistical coordination, the medical decision research, and somehow becoming the family spokesperson for all healthcare communications.

My brother was incredibly involved and helpful, shouldering a lot of the emotional support and daily visits. But somehow, I became the default point person for logistics: coordinating with doctors, making medical decisions, researching treatment options, and managing all healthcare communications. It's like I got appointed Chief Medical Officer without applying for the position.

Extended family members were concerned and wanted updates, but who did they call for information? Me. When it came time to discuss complex treatment options, everyone looked to me like I had suddenly earned a medical degree along with my business credentials.

And here's the part that made me laugh (because if you don't laugh, you'll cry): I started feeling guilty for being the one who could handle everything. Like somehow it was unfair that I understood the medical terms (thanks to ChatGPT), could ask the right questions, and stayed calm during crisis moments. I ended up taking on even more responsibility to compensate for being "too capable."

But those six months also taught me something powerful: You can be incredibly generous and supportive without sacrificing your own well-being or enabling other people's helplessness.

You can love your family deeply while still maintaining boundaries that protect your marriage, your children, your business, and your sanity.

The key is learning the difference between helping and rescuing and understanding that sometimes the most loving thing you can do is refuse to do everything for everyone.

The Success Tax Nobody Warns You About

Here's the truth about something that affects many high-achieving women. The moment you become financially successful, you often inherit the role of family problem solver, emergency fund, and apparently, the personal bank and life support system for everyone who's related to you.

You know what I'm talking about. You work your tail off to build your career, grow your business, and create stability. But instead of being celebrated for your success, you suddenly become responsible for everyone else's problems—financial, emotional, logistical, and everything in between.

It starts subtly. A sibling needs help with a car repair. A cousin asks for a "small loan" for rent. Parents mention struggling with unexpected expenses and also need you to manage their medical appointments. A friend hits a rough patch financially and emotionally, wondering if you could "help them out just this once." Family members assume you'll plan the reunion because "you're so organized" and fund it because "you're doing well."

But somewhere along the line, occasional help becomes expected support. "Small loans" become permanent gifts that nobody intends to repay. You become the default crisis manager, the family event planner, and the one who drops everything when anyone needs anything. Your success has somehow made you responsible for everyone else's emergencies, decisions, and life management.

The guilt is real and complicated. You feel guilty for having more than others—more money, more stability, more capability. Guilty for wanting to protect your own resources, time, and energy. Guilty for feeling resentful when people expect you to solve their problems. Guilty for wondering why your success somehow made you everyone's personal rescue service.

But here's what I want you to understand: Your success doesn't make you obligated to fund everyone else's life or manage their problems. Being good with money and life doesn't mean you're required to be everyone else's safety net. Having resources—whether financial, emotional, or mental—doesn't mean you have to share them with every person who has a sob story and your phone number.

You can be generous without being taken advantage of. You can be supportive without being an enabler. And you can love your family while still protecting your own financial future and sanity.

Meet Brooke: When Caregiving Becomes a Full-Time Job You Didn't Apply For

Brooke is a 35-year-old operations director who went from successful daughter to primary caregiver literally overnight when her father was diagnosed with early-stage dementia.

"I used to call my dad for advice about everything," Brooke told me. "Work decisions, relationship issues, financial planning, he was my sounding board for life. Then one day, he called me three times asking the same question about his insurance, and I realized the roles had completely flipped."

What Brooke didn't expect was how caregiving would affect every other area of her life. Her work performance started suffering because she was constantly distracted by worry and doctor appointments. Her marriage felt the strain of her emotional exhaustion and time commitments. Her three young kids started acting out because Mom was always stressed and distracted.

"I felt like I was failing at everything," Brooke admitted. "I wasn't the operations director I used to be; I wasn't the wife my husband deserved, I wasn't the mother my kids needed, and I definitely wasn't the daughter my father deserved. I was spread so thin that everyone was getting a watered-down version of me."

But the hardest part was the family dynamics. Brooke's siblings had plenty of opinions about their father's care but weren't stepping up to help with the actual work. They criticized her decisions but weren't willing to take on any of the daily responsibilities. And because Brooke was the most organized and financially stable, everyone assumed she should handle all the logistics and expenses too.

"I realized I had become the family's default caregiver not because I was the most qualified, but because I was the most reliable and the most successful," Brooke said. "And honestly, that felt really unfair. Like I was being punished for being competent."

Here's how AI helped Brooke navigate caregiving without losing herself:

Reality Check System: Brooke listed all her caregiving tasks to AI: "I'm managing Dad's medications, driving to all appointments, handling his finances, cooking his meals, and being on-call 24/7 for emergencies." AI helped her categorize: "Which tasks require YOUR specific knowledge? Which could a home health aide handle? What can your father still do independently?"

This revealed that Brooke was doing many things her father could manage on good days, and others that professional services could handle better than an exhausted daughter.

The Delegation Strategy: When Brooke complained to AI, "My siblings say they want to help but never follow through," AI helped her get specific: "Create a shared calendar with concrete tasks. Instead of asking Can you help more? assign specific responsibilities: Michael handles Dad's Tuesday grocery runs, and meal prep. Michele takes Thursday PT appointments and Friday pharmacy pickups. Send this message: I've divided Dad's care needs into specific tasks. Please claim what you can commit to weekly." This eliminated the vague "let me know if you need help" dance.

The Professional Support Network: Brooke told AI: "I can't leave Dad alone but I'm burning out." AI walked her through finding resources: "Search '[your city] adult day programs dementia.' Call your Area Agency on Aging for respite care options. Check if Dad's insurance covers home health aides." AI helped her script calls: "I'm seeking part-time support for my father with early-stage dementia. What programs are available?" Within a week, Brooke had Dad enrolled in a day program three times a week.

The Boundary Scripts: "My sister keeps saying I'm making wrong decisions but won't actually help," Brooke vented to AI. AI provided responses: "When she criticizes, try this: I understand you disagree with using a day program. I'm happy to step back if you'd like to take over Dad's Monday, Wednesday, and Friday care. This puts ownership where it belongs—with the person complaining." Brooke's sister quickly stopped criticizing when faced with actual responsibility.

The Guilt Management Coach: Brooke texted AI at midnight: "Dad called confused and I wasn't there. I'm a terrible daughter." AI reframed: "You've set up professional overnight care precisely for these situations. Ask yourself: Did the system you created work? Was he safe and cared for? Teaching your family to rely on sustainable support systems instead of burning you out means your father will have consistent care for years, not just until you collapse from exhaustion."

Brooke was able to provide excellent oversight of her father's care while reclaiming her effectiveness at work and presence with her family. She learned that being a good daughter didn't require sacrificing everything else she cared about.

"AI helped me realize that caregiving is a marathon, not a sprint," Brooke explains. "I needed systems and support to do it sustainably, not just good intentions and endless guilt."

Meet Patricia: When "You Work for Yourself" Means "You're Always Available"

Patricia, a 47-year-old successful entrepreneur, has been dealing with what she calls "the flexibility myth". This is the assumption that because she owns her own business, she's available to drop everything for family needs at any moment.

My mom calls me at 10 AM on a Tuesday and says, "Can you drive me to my doctor's appointment this afternoon? I know you don't have a real schedule," Patricia told me, shaking her head with a sarcastic smile. "Like running a business is just a hobby I do between family errands."

Patricia's challenge is unique to entrepreneurs: her family sees her flexible schedule as unlimited availability. They assume that because she doesn't have a traditional boss, she can reschedule client meetings, miss important calls, and abandon work projects whenever someone needs a ride, wants company, or has a crisis that requires immediate attention.

"The worst part is the guilt they lay on when I say I can't drop everything," Patricia admitted. "I get responses like, 'But you're your own boss, can't you just move things around?' As if my clients, my income, and my business commitments don't matter because I work from home."

Patricia was also dealing with her mother's increasing health issues and growing dependence on her for everything from technology help to medical advocacy. But instead of planning around Patricia's work schedule, her mother expected Patricia to plan around every medical appointment, grocery run, and social need.

"I realized my family saw my business success as making me more available to them, not less," Patricia said. "They thought because I had financial freedom and schedule flexibility, I should use it all to serve their needs. My boundaries between work and family had completely disappeared."

Here's how AI helped Patricia rebuild boundaries while staying supportive:

The Time Audit Wake-Up Call: Patricia told AI: "I feel like I'm always available but never getting my work done." AI suggested: "Track every family interruption for one week. Log the request, time spent, and impact on your work." The results shocked her: 23 hours of family errands, 7 missed client deadlines, and 3 postponed sales calls. AI presented it starkly: "You're working part-time hours on a full-time business because you're running a free family concierge service. At this rate, what's your projected annual revenue loss?" This data gave Patricia the wake-up call she needed.

The Business Respect Framework: When Patricia's mother said, "But you work from home, you can rearrange things," Patricia asked AI for help. AI provided language: "Tell her: Mom, working from home means my office is here, not that I'm not working. When I'm with clients via Zoom or working on deadlines, it's exactly like being in a corporate office—I can't just leave. Would you ask someone to walk out of a board meeting to run errands?" AI helped her create office hours and an out-of-office message for family that said: "I'm with clients until 5 PM. For non-emergencies, I'll respond after business hours."

The Resource Detective: Patricia's mom called: "I need groceries and a ride to my 2 PM appointment." Instead of dropping everything, Patricia typed to AI: "Find senior services in [zip code] that can help today." Within minutes, AI provided: "Instacart delivers in 2 hours. Uber Health provides medical transportation. Your local Area Agency on Aging offers free senior shuttle service—here's the number." Patricia could solve the problem in 10 minutes instead of losing half her workday.

The Emergency vs. Convenience Filter: Patricia asked AI: "How do I know when to drop everything versus when to say no?" AI helped her create clear criteria: "True emergencies: hospitalization, falls, urgent medical issues—drop everything. Convenience requests: routine appointments, grocery runs, loneliness, wanting company—offer alternatives. Test each request: Would I leave a crucial client meeting for this? If not, it's not an emergency." This framework removed guilt from her decision-making.

The Boundary Education Coach: When her brother said, "Must be nice to make your own schedule," Patricia asked AI for a response. AI suggested: "Use this as a teaching moment: Actually, successful entrepreneurs have less flexibility because we're accountable to multiple clients instead of one boss. When I miss a deadline, I lose income and reputation. Let me show you my calendar so you can see why I need advance notice for family requests." This reframed her boundaries as business education rather than rejection.

The shift was liberating. Patricia stopped being the family's on-call service provider and started being a successful entrepreneur who could also be a loving, supportive daughter and family member, on terms that worked for everyone.

"AI helped me understand that having a flexible schedule doesn't mean having no schedule," Patricia explains. "I could be generous with my time while still protecting the business that allowed me to be generous in the first place."

How I Use AI for Family Relationships That Actually Work

Here are a few ways AI helps me stay connected to my family while protecting my own peace of mind:

The Love vs. Logic Filter: When my mom asks me to visit three times a week because "good daughters make time for their mothers," I share this with AI: "How do I handle the guilt when she makes it about being a good daughter?" AI helps me see the pattern: "Notice she's connecting your love to a specific action (visits) rather than acknowledging all the ways you show care. This is emotional pressure, not a reflection of your actual relationship quality." AI helps me respond: "Mom, I love you so much. With the kids' schedules and my business commitments, three visits weekly isn't sustainable. How about we make our monthly lunch dates special, and I'll come visit once a week. Quality time matters more than quantity." This helps me offer meaningful connection without overwhelming my schedule.

The Empowerment Strategy: When a friend calls crying about her job, my instinct is to solve everything. I ask AI: "How do I help without taking over?" AI provides coaching questions: "Instead of giving advice, ask: What options are you considering? What's worked for you in similar situations before? What would you tell a friend in this position?" Now, instead of my usual tendency to map out her entire career strategy, I ask these questions. It's amazing how often people talk themselves into their own solutions—and feel proud of figuring it out themselves.

The Graceful No Toolkit: My extended family wanted me to host the family reunion BBQ at my house during my busiest season because "you have such a beautiful space." I type to AI: "How do I redirect this without offending everyone?" AI provides scripts: "I'm honored you want to gather at our home. Unfortunately, that timeframe is my peak work season. What if we rent the community center at the park? It has a full kitchen, covered pavilion, and the kids would love the playground. I'm happy to research venues and share options with everyone." AI helps me offer solutions without sacrificing my schedule, showing I care about the reunion while protecting my boundaries.

The Perspective Shift: When I'm feeling guilty because my parents are getting older and I can't spend unlimited time with them, I tell AI: "I feel like a terrible daughter. They won't be here forever and I'm always too busy." AI reframes: "You're carrying guilt about time you don't have instead of maximizing the time you do have. What if quality matters more than quantity? List the meaningful ways you connect with them now—your daily calls, weekly visits, monthly lunches, sharing photos of the kids. Being a good daughter means showing up authentically when you can, not burning yourself out trying to stop time." This helps me focus on creating meaningful moments instead of drowning in guilt about what's not possible.

The Hidden Cost of Being Everyone's Everything

There is a heavy toll that constantly caring for everyone else takes on your own life, relationships, and well-being.

When you're the family's go-to person for everything, it affects your marriage because your husband watches you give your best energy to everyone else's problems. It impacts your children because they see Mom always stressed about other people's crises. It hurts your business because you're constantly distracted by family drama that you can't solve.

But the biggest cost is what it does to your own sense of identity and purpose. You start defining your worth by how much you can do for other people instead of what you're building for yourself. You measure your success by whether everyone else is happy instead of whether you're fulfilled.

The beautiful truth is this: You can be a loving, supportive family member without being everyone's personal crisis manager, financial advisor, and emotional support system. In fact, helping people develop their own coping skills is often more loving than doing everything for them.

When you set healthy boundaries, amazing things happen. Your family members become more capable and confident. Your marriage gets more of your attention and energy. Your children see a model of a woman who values herself and her commitments. Your business thrives because you're not constantly distracted by other people's emergencies.

AI helps with family dynamics by:

- Helping you distinguish between helping and enabling
- Providing scripts for setting boundaries that protect relationships
- Teaching you to delegate responsibilities instead of handling everything yourself
- Reminding you that your own well-being matters too
- Helping you identify when professional support is needed instead of family intervention

She Leads as a Daughter & Caregiver

I'M FAILING EVERYONE TRYING TO CARE FOR KIDS AND AGING PARENTS

AI HELPS ME COORDINATE CARE SO EVERYONE FEELS SUPPORTED

💬 TAKE A PAUSE, FRIEND

Before we dive into practical applications, pour yourself some tea and honestly think about these questions:

1. What family responsibilities have you taken on because you're "good at them" versus because no one else will step up? Which ones could be shared or delegated?
2. How has being the successful one in your family affected your relationships with relatives? Do people treat you differently because of your financial stability or professional success?
3. When was the last time you asked your family for support instead of always being the one providing it? What stops you from reaching out when you need help?
4. What would happen if you weren't available to solve a family crisis immediately? Are you preventing your loved ones from developing their own problem-solving skills?
5. If you could redesign your family relationships to be more balanced and reciprocal, what would that look like?

Your answers will help you identify where you might need better boundaries and more sustainable ways of supporting your family without sacrificing yourself.

Beyond Rescue Mode: AI for Sustainable Family Support

While helping family members is part of loving relationships, AI's real power lies in teaching you how to support people in ways that build their capacity rather than increasing their dependence on you.

Empowerment Planning: AI helps you shift from solving problems for family members to coaching them through developing their own solutions and capabilities.

Resource Connection: AI identifies professional services, community resources, and support systems that can provide help without everything falling on your shoulders.

Boundary Communication: AI provides loving language for setting limits on what support you can provide while maintaining strong relationships.

Crisis Prevention: AI helps you spot patterns in family crises and address underlying issues instead of just responding to emergencies.

Self-Care Integration: AI reminds you that taking care of yourself isn't selfish—it's essential for being able to support others sustainably over the long term.

DO THIS NOW, NOT LATER

Ready to use AI for healthier family dynamics? Choose one experiment to try this week:

Option 1: The Independence Shift Choose one way you currently help a family member and ask AI: "How can I transform this from doing it for them to empowering them to do it themselves?" For example, if you manage your mom's online banking, ask AI to help you create a simple guide to teach her instead. This week, pick one area where you can shift from rescuer to teacher.

Option 2: The Boundary Conversation Choose one family relationship where you need clearer limits and ask AI: "Help me prepare a loving conversation about what support I can realistically provide and what they need to handle themselves." Have this conversation within the week.

Option 3: The Resource Research Pick one area where family members frequently need your help and ask AI: "Help me find professional resources or community services that could provide this support instead of me always being the solution." Share these resources with your family.

Choose the option that feels most relevant to your current family situation and commit to trying it consistently for one week.

CHAPTER 14 QUICK REFERENCE

Key Mindset Shift: Supporting your family doesn't mean sacrificing yourself—healthy families build each other's capacity rather than draining one person

Core Truth: You can love your family deeply while still protecting your own well-being, resources, and priorities

Action Step: Choose one AI family boundary experiment to try consistently for one week

Remember: The best gift you can give your family is modeling how to be a strong, capable person who can handle challenges while still being generous and supportive

> Being the successful one doesn't mean carrying everyone else. It means knowing when to help and when to empower.
>
> — T. Reneé Smith

CHAPTER 15

SHE LEADS AS A FRIEND & COMMUNITY MEMBER

> "Community is created one authentic connection at a time."
> – T. Reneé Smith

The Day I Realized I Was Surrounded by People but Felt Alone

I was lounging on my couch one Saturday afternoon, mindlessly scrolling through Instagram while my family moved around me. The house was full of life—kids laughing, my husband working on something in the garage, the peaceful feeling of a blessed life.

So why did I feel so incredibly lonely?

My thumb moved on autopilot, double-tapping photos of women I called friends. There was Kim's beach getaway with her sorority girlfriends—matching swimsuits and champagne toasts. Jennifer's impromptu girls' night—faces glowing with laughter and too much wine. Another friend's Sunday brunch crew, same women every month, inside jokes I'd never understand.

With each scroll, my craving for real girlfriend connection intensified. I was witnessing their friendships from behind a screen, hitting heart emojis on moments I'd never be part of. When they posted about "sisters by choice" and "my ride or ride"—and yes, I'm that person who says "ride or ride" because why are we dying? We're thriving, thank you very much—I realized I wasn't anybody's ride or ride anymore.

When was the last time a girlfriend randomly showed up at my door just to check on me? When did I last ugly-cry to someone who wasn't my husband? When did I have a conversation that went so deep we forgot to check our phones, lost track of time, and ended up solving the world's problems over tea?

I couldn't remember.

That night, feeling a genuine desire for real connection, I found myself typing questions to AI that I was too embarrassed to ask anyone else: "Is it normal for successful women to wake up one day and realize they don't have many deep friendships? Sure, I have friends I grab lunch or dinner with, but where are my sister girlfriends, the ones doing life alongside me? How did I become the woman who has everything except someone to call when I need to hear someone say, 'me too'? I've spent so many years building my empire that I forgot to build my tribe. How do I find genuine sisterhood when everyone already has their core people? I want friends who know when I'm struggling behind my smile, not just surface-level connections who comment goals on my posts."

AI helped me realize I wasn't alone. Ambitious women everywhere were asking the same questions I was—how did I become so successful yet so disconnected from meaningful friendship?

The Surface-Level Friendship Trap

We need to address what happens to friendships when life gets complicated and success demands increase.

In your twenties, friendship feels effortless. You have time for three-hour phone calls, spontaneous girls' nights, weekend adventures, and those deep conversations that happen over wine and vulnerability. You're there for each other through dating drama, career uncertainties, and life's beautiful messiness.

Then life happens. Your thirties, forties, fifties, sixties, and beyond.

Here's what people rarely talk about: This isn't just about being busy. It's about forgetting that friendship requires the same intentional cultivation as any other important relationship.

And here's where AI becomes unexpectedly powerful for friendships: it can help you move beyond surface-level interactions to create the deep, authentic connections your soul craves, even during your busiest seasons.

The Investment vs. Availability Myth

I used to think being a good friend meant being constantly available—responding to every text immediately, saying yes to every invitation, being the one everyone could count on for everything.

But here's what I learned: Great friendship isn't about perfect availability. It's about intentional presence and meaningful investment.

Your friends don't need you to be constantly accessible. They need you to show up fully when you are together, remember what matters to them, and invest in the relationship with the same strategic thinking you bring to other important areas of your life.

My Journey from Lonely to Connected

Here's the truth about my friendship journey: I had several friend groups. The AAU tournament moms who survived competition season together. The carpool warriors who knew exactly which Starbucks could get us through the pickup line fastest. The school volunteer moms who planned every end-of-year party, organized teacher appreciation week, and somehow made 200 handcrafted carnival prizes look effortless.

We'd get together for brunches where the mimosas flowed freely (even though I'd stick to water), girls' dinners where we'd laugh until our faces hurt, and the occasional weekend trip where we'd pretend we were twenty-five again (until 10 PM when we all wanted to go to bed). These women were wonderful, and those gatherings were fun.

But as our kids got older and scattered to different schools, travel teams, and interests, our connections started fading. The group chat that used to blow up daily became monthly check-ins. The mom I used to see at practice became someone I'd run into at the grocery store and promise to "get together soon"—which we both knew was code for "see you in six months at another grocery store run."

I realized these friendships, while meaningful during that season, weren't necessarily aligned with where I was going in life. We'd bonded over our kids' activities, but now I was craving connections with women who understood building a business while raising a family. Who got the tension of having dreams bigger than the school fundraiser (though respect to those PTA presidents—y'all are the real MVPs).

My Heartfelt Prayer to God

One night during my prayer time, I asked God to bring me the kind of friendships I was craving. His response surprised me: "Create what you're seeking. Build what you wish existed."

I literally laughed out loud. "Lord, have you seen my schedule? I can barely maintain the friendships I have, and you want me to build a whole community?"

But the nudge wouldn't go away. For years, I put that calling on ice. I was too busy, convinced I wasn't the right person for this, and honestly, I wanted to join something that already existed, not build something from scratch. I was already building too many things—my business, my family, my sanity. The last thing I needed was another project. But God's whispers turned into shouts, and the longing in my heart became impossible to ignore. So, I finally surrendered and did what any modern woman does when God gives her a vision—I asked AI for help.

"Help me understand what ambitious women really need in different life stages," I typed.

AI walked me through the journey: The twenty-something go-getter trying to build her career or business while everyone's getting married. The thirty-something navigating fertility decisions, new motherhood, or choosing to be child-free while building her empire. The forty-something who might be having her first baby, raising teenagers, or launching her next big venture—wondering if she's just getting started. The fifty-something redefining success on her own terms, whether her kids are in college or elementary school. The sixty-something powerhouse whose kids might finally be leaving home—or who's raising grandkids. The seventy-plus force of nature who refuses to be invisible just because society says she should slow down.

Then I asked: "What would make these women feel like they found their tribe, not just another community where everyone's pretending to have it all together?"

AI's response made me tear up: "They want a place to celebrate without being called boastful or arrogant. To fail without being judged. To cry without being weak. To laugh without explanation. They want to be known for who they are, not what they've achieved or what they do. They want friends who see their heart, not just their highlight reel."

"So basically," I typed back, "they want what I want—real friends who get that I can inspire my team to exceed quarterly goals but can't inspire my kids to put their dishes in the dishwasher."

That's when the She Leads and She Loves movement was born—not from a business strategy but from my own authentic prayer for sisterhood. It became the answer to what I was seeking: a space where ambitious women could be fully themselves. Where you can share that you crushed your quarterly goals AND that you're struggling in your marriage. Where admitting you don't have it all figured out is met with "Girl, same" not judgment.

The goal was to create gatherings where professional wins get celebrated alongside personal victories. Where learning to set boundaries with your mother-in-law gets as much support as launching your new product line. Where we understand that sometimes the biggest achievement of the day is not losing it on your kids (and if you did, we've got grace for that too).

AI helped me brainstorm ideas to make it to feel like home—monthly virtual tea or coffee dates where we show up in our real lives (messy buns welcome), quarterly in-person gatherings where deep conversation flows, and a text thread where we share the real stuff, not the Instagram version.

It is exactly what I was craving all along—women who text "how did the meeting go?" and want the real answer. Who remember your mom's surgery date. Who celebrate your wins like they're their own. Who show up with wine and wisdom when life gets hard.

Because here's what I learned: When women support each other authentically—when we stop pretending and start connecting—we don't just succeed. We soar. Together.

She Leads as a Friend & Community Member

Panel 1: A woman stands near a birthday cake and balloons, looking distressed, saying "I'M TOO BUSY TO MAINTAIN MEANINGFUL FRIENDSHIPS" while another couple takes selfies nearby.

Panel 2: A woman sits on a couch gesturing toward an AI device on a side table, saying "AI HELPS ME NURTURE DEEP CONNECTIONS THAT MATTER."

> 💬 **TAKE A PAUSE, FRIEND**
>
> Before we dive into practical strategies, take some time to honestly assess your current friendship landscape:
>
> 1. When was the last time you had a genuine girlfriend moment? Not a scheduled meeting, but a spontaneous, soul-nourishing connection with a friend?
> 2. How many of your current friendships would you describe as deep and authentic versus surface-level and obligatory?
> 3. If you could have three deep, supportive friendships, what would those relationships look like? What would you give and receive?
> 4. What prevents you from investing in friendships the way you invest in other important relationships?
> 5. Are your current friendships aligned with who you're becoming, or are they mostly tied to who you used to be?

AI as Your Friendship Enhancement Partner

Think of AI as your relationship coordination system that helps you show up as the friend you want to be:

- Helps identify which friendships align with your current life direction and values
- Suggests meaningful activities based on friends' interests and current situations

- Reminds you of important dates and ongoing situations so you can follow up meaningfully
- Provides conversation starters that create opportunities for deeper sharing
- Helps you understand different communication styles so you can connect more effectively
- Offers ideas for meaningful gestures that show you care

Real-World AI Friendship Applications

Friendship Alignment Check "I have several friend groups from different life seasons. How do I identify which relationships to invest in more deeply?" AI helps you evaluate: Which friends celebrate your growth? Who's interested in where you're going, not just where you've been? Which relationships energize versus drain you?

Meaningful Check-Ins Instead of generic "how are you?" texts, ask AI: "My friend is dealing with her dad's illness. What would be a meaningful way to check in?" AI might suggest: "I've been thinking about you since you mentioned your dad's diagnosis. How did his appointment with the specialist go?"

Creating Your Tribe "I want to build a community of ambitious women who support each other authentically. How do I start?" AI helps you identify women in your life who might crave the same connection, suggests ways to test the waters with small gatherings, and provides frameworks for creating safe spaces where women can be real.

DO THIS NOW, NOT LATER

Ready to transform your friendships from surface-level to soul-deep? Choose one action to take this week:

Action 1: Reconnect with One Core Friend Choose the friend you miss most but have let slip into surface-level contact. Ask AI to help you craft a message that shows you've been thinking about them specifically. Plan a meaningful activity together that creates space for real conversation.

Action 2: Start a Community Tradition Use AI to plan a gathering for your friend group that encourages deeper sharing. Create a regular tradition that everyone can look forward to and prioritize. Focus on activities that bring out authentic conversation and mutual support.

Action 3: Become a Better Support System Think of a friend who's facing a challenge. Ask AI to help you understand specific ways to support them beyond generic offers of help. Take action on one concrete way to show up for them this week.

A COACH'S NOTE

Friend, I know this chapter might bring up some tender feelings about friendships you've let slip or connections you've been craving. Maybe you're feeling guilty about not being the friend you want to be, or maybe you're feeling lonely despite being surrounded by people.

Here's what I want you to know: Recognizing that you want deeper friendship is the first step toward creating it. The fact that you're reading this means you value connection and community, and that's beautiful.

You don't need to be perfect to be a good friend. You don't need unlimited time or energy to create meaningful connections. You just need to be intentional about the relationships that matter to you and consistent in showing up for them.

Start where you are, with the people you have, and let AI help you show up as the friend you want to be. Community is created one authentic connection at a time, and every small gesture of genuine care contributes to building something beautiful.

CHAPTER 15 QUICK REFERENCE

Key Mindset Shifts:

- Friendship requires intentional investment, not just availability
- Deep connections are built through consistent, meaningful interactions
- Supporting others effectively requires understanding their specific needs

AI Friendship Applications:

- Meaningful check-ins based on friends' current situations
- Friendship alignment evaluation for life seasons
- Community building frameworks

Your Action Step: Choose one friendship to invest in meaningfully this week

Remember: Community is created one authentic connection at a time.

> Success without sisterhood is just expensive loneliness. Build your tribe with the same intention you built your empire.
>
> — T. RENEÉ SMITH

CHAPTER 16

SHE LEADS AS A PROFESSIONAL

> *"Your career is a platform for your purpose. Use it wisely."*
> – T. Reneé Smith

The Boardroom Where Everything Clicked

I was sitting across from Denise, a Senior Vice President at a major financial firm, who looked like she hadn't slept in weeks. She'd hired me to help her prepare for the most important presentation of her career—a board proposal that could reshape how her company developed emerging leaders.

"I have three days," she said, sliding a mountain of research across the table. "Legal needs to review on Thursday, and I present Friday morning. I've been working on this for two months, but it's still not right."

I looked at her exhausted face and saw myself from years ago—believing that professional excellence meant personally grinding through every detail. But my deep dive into AI's capabilities had revealed a different path.

"What if we could get you ready in three hours, not three weeks?" I asked.

She laughed. Then realized I was serious. "The look on her face was priceless—somewhere between 'Is this woman crazy?' and 'Please, God, let her be right because I haven't seen my kids awake in three days.'"

Together, we fed her research into AI—employee engagement surveys, leadership development studies, competitor programs, and industry best practices. But instead of asking AI to write her presentation, we asked it to identify patterns and connections human analysis might miss.

AI found something remarkable: Their highest-potential employees who left within two years all mentioned the same thing in exit interviews—not money, not work-life balance, but lack of strategic thinking opportunities. They were drowning in execution and starving for innovation time.

That insight transformed Denise's entire proposal. Instead of a traditional leadership development program, she proposed an "Innovation Lab" where emerging leaders would spend 20% of their time on strategic projects with C-suite visibility.

Three hours later, Denise had a compelling presentation that would normally have taken weeks to develop. But more importantly, she had confidence backed by data and insights, not exhaustion.

Friday afternoon, she texted me: "They approved everything. And they want me to lead the entire initiative. This changes my whole career trajectory."

The Leadership Paradox That's Holding You Back

After researching AI's impact on careers, I discovered that most times the higher you climb in leadership, the less time you spend leading.

Think about it. You got promoted because of your strategic thinking, innovative solutions, and ability to inspire teams. But what percentage of your day do you spend on those high-value activities now?

If you're like most leaders, you're trapped in what I call "leadership quicksand"—drowning in reports, status meetings, email chains, and administrative tasks that multiply with each promotion. You're so busy managing the mechanics of leadership that you don't have time to lead.

Here's the kicker: While you're stuck in reactive mode, other leaders are using AI to revolutionize how they work. They're not smarter than you—they're just more leveraged. They've figured out that AI can handle the management so they can focus on the leadership.

Maria's 90-Day Leadership Breakthrough

Let me share how Maria transformed from an exhausted Director of Operations to a visionary leader being fast-tracked for VP—using AI to finally unlock the strategic thinker she'd always been.

Maria, 47, was drowning in the details despite her brilliance. "I'm the first one in and the last one out," she told me during our first coaching session, her voice cracking with exhaustion. "My boss keeps saying I need to be more strategic, but I'm literally in back-to-back meetings from 7 AM to 6 PM. When I get home, I have nothing left—not for my husband, not for my friends, not even for myself. I'm failing at everything that matters."

Her breaking point came during a performance review that felt like a punch to the gut: "Strong executor but needs to demonstrate more strategic vision." Maria sat in her car afterward and cried. She knew she had vision—she'd lie awake at night thinking of innovative solutions. She just never had time to develop or share them.

"I felt like I was slowly disappearing," Maria told me. "The strategic, creative parts of me were dying under spreadsheets and status reports."

That's when she agreed to try my 90-day AI integration experiment:

Week 1-2: The Reality Maria tracked every task for two weeks, then had AI categorize them. The results saddened her: 65% of her time went to tasks AI could handle—data analysis, report generation, meeting summaries, status updates. "I have a master's degree," she said through tears, "and I'm basically a glorified administrator."

Week 3-4: The Fear and Freedom She started using AI to automate routine analyses and create first-draft reports. Her initial fear was visceral: "What if I become replaceable?" But something happened—AI caught patterns she'd been too overwhelmed to notice, like inventory inefficiencies that she'd sensed but never had time to investigate.

Week 5-8: The Woman She'd Forgotten With 10+ hours freed weekly, Maria instituted what she called "Vision Mornings"—sacred time for strategic thinking. "I felt like I was meeting myself again," she shared. "The Maria who had ideas, who could see possibilities, who remembered why she chose this career."

She used AI to research industry innovations and model operational improvements, but more importantly, she had space to think creatively again.

Week 9-12: The Recognition She'd Craved Maria began presenting insights, not just updates, in leadership meetings. When she proposed an AI-enhanced supply chain system projected to save $2M annually, her CEO pulled her aside: "This is the leader we knew you could be."

The Result: Her next review included the words "ready for VP-level responsibilities." But here's what made Maria cry happy tears—she was home for dinner with her husband four nights a week, present and energized, not depleted and distracted.

"I thought using AI meant losing my personal touch," Maria told me six months later, her eyes bright with purpose. "Instead, it gave me back my humanity. I'm a better leader AND a better mother because I'm not exhausted all the time. I finally feel like myself again."

The transformation went beyond professional success. Her husband told her, "You're like the woman I married again—excited about life." She started mentoring young women in her company, something she'd always wanted to do but never had time for. She even joined a book club, rediscovering passions outside of work.

"AI didn't make me replaceable," Maria explained. "It made me remember why I'm irreplaceable—my ability to see connections, inspire teams, and create vision. I just needed space to let those gifts shine."

She Leads as a Professional

💭 TAKE A PAUSE, FRIEND

Before diving into strategies, let's get honest about your professional reality:

1. What percentage of your day is spent on work that showcases your leadership versus work that just keeps things running?

2. When was the last time you had two uninterrupted hours to think strategically about your department or team?
3. If AI could give you back 10 hours per week, what leadership activities would you finally have time for?
4. What's one innovative idea you've had but haven't been able to develop because you're too busy with day-to-day management?
5. Are you being paid for your strategic thinking or your ability to process information?

Professional AI Strategies for Leaders

Here are foundational ways women leaders are using AI to reclaim their actual jobs:

1. **The Decision Intelligence System** Stop drowning in data and start surfacing insights. Feed AI your reports, metrics, and analyses with specific prompts that extract what matters.

    Example: Lisa, a Marketing Director, uploads her weekly campaign data and asks: "Analyze this campaign data and identify: 1) Any metrics performing 20% above or below average, 2) Patterns that predict customer conversion, 3) Which decisions need my immediate attention vs. what's running smoothly." She now spends 30 minutes on what used to take 4 hours.

2. **The Meeting Multiplier Method** Transform meetings from time-sinks into strategic accelerators using AI to prepare and follow up.

   Example: Kim's weekly 2-hour team meetings became 45-minute strategic sessions. She prompts AI: "Based on these project updates, create: 1) A 5-bullet executive summary of progress, 2) Three strategic questions we need to discuss synchronously, 3) Action items that can be handled asynchronously." Her team loves the focused, productive meetings.

3. **The Communication Efficiency Framework** Let AI handle routine communications while you focus on messages requiring emotional intelligence.

   Example: Director of HR Michelle prompts AI: "Draft a professional but warm email announcing our new flexible work policy. Include: key changes, implementation date, and where to find details. Tone: supportive and clear, acknowledging employee's concerns and feedback." She then personalizes it with specific examples and empathy only she can provide.

4. **The Talent Development Accelerator** Use AI to personalize development plans while you focus on high-impact mentoring.

   Example: Regional Manager Keisha manages 30+ team members. She prompts AI: "Analyze these performance reviews and identify: 1) Top 3 development areas for each person, 2) Which employees show leadership potential, 3) Suggested learning resources matched to each person's learning style." This gives her targeted coaching points for one-on-ones.

5. **The Innovation Time Creator** Systematically use AI to buy back time for strategic thinking.

   Example: CFO Patricia blocks "Vision Mornings" twice weekly. She prompts AI: "Analyze these financial reports and create: 1) One-page executive summary highlighting key trends, 2) Areas requiring CFO-level decision, 3) Routine items that are tracking to plan. Flag only exceptions needing my attention." This freed 8 hours weekly for strategic planning.

Advanced Professional Strategies for Leaders

Ready to differentiate yourself as a next-level leader? Here's how:

1. **The Predictive Leadership Model** Use AI to anticipate challenges before they become crises.

   Implementation: Feed AI your data and prompt: "Based on these industry trends, team performance metrics, and market indicators, identify: 1) Potential risks in the next 3-6 months, 2) Early warning signals to watch, 3) Proactive strategies to address each risk before it materializes."

2. **The Cross-Functional Intelligence Network** Connect dots across silos by synthesizing information from different departments.

   Implementation: Upload reports from various departments and prompt: "Analyze these reports from sales, marketing, operations, and finance. Identify: 1) Hidden connections between departments, 2) Opportunities for collaboration that could improve outcomes, 3) Conflicting strategies that need alignment."

3. **The Stakeholder Influence Maximizer** Adapt your communication to different leadership styles.

   Implementation: Before presentations, prompt AI: "Review these successful past presentations to [Executive Name]. Identify: 1) What data types they respond to best, 2) Their typical questions or concerns, 3) Communication style preferences. Suggest how to adapt my presentation accordingly."

4. **The Strategic Initiative Accelerator** Launch initiatives faster with AI-powered research and planning.

   Implementation: When proposing new initiatives, prompt: "Research best practices for [specific initiative type] in [industry]. Provide: 1) Top 5 success factors from similar implementations, 2) Common pitfalls and how to avoid them, 3) A phased implementation roadmap with milestones and metrics."

5. **The Executive Presence Amplifier** Prepare for every executive interaction with strategic insights.

   Implementation: Before leadership meetings, prompt: "Connect my department's current projects to the company's stated strategic objectives. Show: 1) How our work drives corporate goals, 2) Metrics that demonstrate strategic impact, 3) Insights about future opportunities that align with company vision."

Real-World Implementation Examples

The Director Who Became the Youngest VP Amanda, 34, used AI to analyze her company's digital transformation efforts across departments. She identified integration opportunities that would save $5M annually, presenting a unified strategy that got her promoted over candidates with 10+ more years of experience.

The Manager Who Transformed Team Performance Carol used AI to analyze her team's work patterns and identified that highest performers spent 60% more time on strategic projects. She restructured workflows to give everyone more strategic time, improving team performance metrics by 40% in six months.

The Leader Who Prevented a Crisis Jennifer used AI to analyze customer service patterns and predicted a major satisfaction crisis three months before it would have exploded. Her proactive solution saved the company millions and established her as a strategic thinker.

DO THIS NOW, NOT LATER

Choose your starting point for AI-enhanced leadership:

Action 1: The Leadership Time Audit Track your time for one week. Have AI categorize activities as "Strategic Leadership" (only you can do), "Management Tasks" (AI can enhance), or "Administrative Work" (AI can handle). Commit to delegating one administrative task this week.

Action 2: The Strategic Visibility Project Choose one upcoming leadership presentation. Use AI to prepare with strategic insights, not just updates. Notice how differently you're perceived when you lead with vision.

Action 3: The Innovation Hour Experiment Block one hour this week for strategic thinking. Use AI to handle whatever would normally fill that time. Use the hour to develop one innovative idea for your team or department.

Action 4: The Meeting Revolution Test Pick your most time-consuming recurring meeting. Use AI to analyze what needs synchronous discussion versus what could be handled asynchronously. Propose a new format that cuts meeting time by 40%.

A COACH'S NOTE

Friend, can I be honest? I used to be that leader who wore exhaustion like a badge of honor. I'd brag about my 80-hour weeks like it was an Olympic medal. I later came to realize there's no gold medal for burnout, just medical bills and regret."

I know this chapter might have surfaced frustrations about how you're spending your professional energy. Maybe you're realizing how much of your leadership potential is buried under busywork or feeling angry about the gap between the leader you want to be and the administrator you've become.

Here's what matters: You haven't been failing—you've been surviving in a system that confuses busy with productive, presence with impact, and effort with value.

Your organization didn't promote you to process emails faster or create prettier reports. They promoted you because they saw leadership potential—strategic thinking, innovation capability, the ability to inspire and guide others toward meaningful outcomes.

AI doesn't replace those leadership qualities. It reveals them by clearing away everything that's been hiding your true value.

Start small. Pick one routine task that frustrates you every week and hand it to AI. Use that reclaimed time to do something that reminds you why you wanted to lead in the first place.

The future belongs to leaders who combine technological leverage with human wisdom. Who use AI to handle management so they can focus on leadership. Who understand that their value isn't in doing everything—it's in doing what matters most.

That leader? She's you, waiting to be unleashed.

CHAPTER 16 QUICK REFERENCE

Key Mindset Shifts:

- Your value as a leader lies in vision and strategy, not task execution
- AI handles management so you can focus on leadership
- Strategic thinking time is not a luxury—it's a necessity
- Being busy is not the same as being impactful

Professional AI Strategies:

- Decision Intelligence System—surface insights from data
- Meeting Multiplier Method—transform time-sinks into strategic value
- Communication Efficiency Framework—focus on high-impact messages
- Talent Development Accelerator—personalize growth at scale
- Innovation Time Creator—systematically reclaim strategic thinking time

Advanced Strategies:

- Predictive Leadership Model—anticipate challenges before they emerge
- Cross-Functional Intelligence Network—connect dots across silos

- Stakeholder Influence Maximizer—adapt to different leadership styles
- Strategic Initiative Accelerator—compress planning timelines
- Executive Presence Amplifier—always show up with insights

Your Action Step: Choose one routine professional task to delegate to AI this week, then reinvest that time in strategic thinking

Remember: Your career is a platform for your purpose. Use it wisely.

> Your brilliance isn't in doing everything—it's in knowing what only you can do.
>
> —T. Reneé Smith

CHAPTER 17

SHE LEADS AS A CEO & BUSINESS OWNER

> *"Your business should serve your life, not consume it."*
> – T. Reneé Smith

The Three-Year Deal That Almost Stole My Soul

I was reviewing a government RFP for strategic planning consulting—exactly the type of work my team and I had been doing successfully for years. This contract would guarantee three years of steady revenue, and my team was excited as they strategized our response.

This RFP felt different. I wasn't excited about the opportunity like I had been in the past. For months, I'd been sensing God nudging me in a different direction. Every prayer, every quiet moment pointed toward leadership development and facilitating small business accelerators. But every RFP that landed on my desk was for Strategic planning and Government consulting. The very work I felt like God was pivoting me from.

"This is perfect for us," my project manager said, already calculating our win probability. "We could nail this proposal."

She was right. We were good at this work—really good. We had the track record, the references, the expertise. This RFP was practically written for us.

But I knew in my gut this wasn't what I was supposed to be doing in this season.

The problem? I had zero tangible evidence to support my feeling. No data showing leadership development would be more profitable. No guarantees that small business accelerators would sustain us. Just this persistent whisper in my spirit saying, "This isn't your path in this season."

I'd made this mistake before—choosing the money over the divine direction I was being led toward. Every single time, it came with a heavy price: late nights that stretched into early mornings, stress that lived in my shoulders like a permanent resident, and that hollow feeling of building something that paid the bills but starved my purpose.

"We're not pursuing this RFP," I announced to my team the next morning.

The silence was thick. I watched confusion ripple across their faces, followed by barely concealed frustration. How could I explain that God was redirecting our entire business model when the spreadsheets said to stay the course?

"But this would be guaranteed revenue," someone finally said. "This is what we do best."

"I know," I replied, my voice steadier than my resolve. "But it's not what we're supposed to do next."

That's when entrepreneurship got really real. It's one thing to follow your purpose when the path is profitable. It's another thing entirely to choose faith over financial security, especially when you're responsible for other people's livelihoods.

For three days, I second-guessed myself. What kind of CEO turns down potential money for an uncertain calling? What if I was wrong? What if this wasn't God but just my own restlessness?

But then I remembered every time I'd chosen money over mission. The exhaustion. The resentment. The slow death of passion that happens when you're building something that's profitable but not purposeful.

What I discovered through that soul-searching didn't just change that one decision—it shifted my entire approach to building a business that creates both wealth and wellness.

We didn't pursue the government RFP. Instead, I spent the next year completely pivoting our business model toward leadership development and small business acceleration. I learned to delegate, automate, and eventually leverage AI to handle the operational work that had been consuming my life.

Three years later, the same timeframe that government contract would have taken—my company was aligned with work that lit me up instead of burning me out. More importantly, I was building programs that transformed lives, working with leaders and entrepreneurs who wanted real change, and creating a legacy rather than just a living.

That's when I learned a valuable lesson about entrepreneurship: The goal isn't to build a business that makes you rich and miserable. It's to build a business that makes you wealthy in every way that matters.

The CEO Trap Nobody Warns You About

Let's talk about what happens to many women entrepreneurs as their businesses grow. We start with beautiful visions of freedom, flexibility, and financial independence. We want to build something meaningful while being present for our families and communities.

But somewhere between startup and scale-up, many of us get trapped in what I call the "Indispensable CEO Syndrome."

You become the bottleneck in your own business. Every decision needs your approval. Every client wants to work directly with you. Every problem becomes your emergency. Every growth opportunity requires more of your personal time and energy.

You're working harder than you ever worked for someone else, but now the pressure never stops because there's no one above you to make the hard decisions. You're successful on paper but exhausted in reality.

Here's what we rarely hear about business growth: If scaling your business requires scaling your stress, you're building wrong.

And here's where AI becomes revolutionary for women business owners: **it can help you build systems that scale your impact without scaling your involvement, creating the kind of business that serves your life instead of consuming it.**

Why Women Entrepreneurs Need This More Than Anyone

Women face unique challenges in business ownership that make AI support not just helpful, but essential:

The Superwoman Expectation: Society expects women business owners to excel professionally while maintaining perfect families, communities, and personal lives. AI can help you manage multiple roles without burning out.

The Relationship-Heavy Business Model: Women often build businesses that depend heavily on personal relationships and individual attention. AI can help maintain that personal touch while creating scalable systems.

The Underestimation Factor: Women entrepreneurs often face more scrutiny and have to prove themselves repeatedly. AI can help you consistently deliver exceptional results that speak for themselves.

The Capital Access Challenge: Women receive less venture capital and business funding, making efficient operations and smart growth strategies essential. AI can help you achieve more with fewer resources.

The Values-Integration Need: Women want businesses that align with their values and support their communities. AI can help you scale impact alongside income.

Rachel's PR Story: When AI Threatened Everything She'd Built

Rachel, a PR agency owner, thought AI would destroy her business. "I spent 15 years perfecting my craft," Rachel told me. "Learning which journalists prefer which angles. Building relationships that get emails opened instead of deleted. Understanding the subtle psychology of a perfect pitch. And then I watched AI write a press release in 30 seconds that would have taken me two hours."

The fear in her eyes was something I recognized—because I'd felt it too. It was the fear of becoming obsolete. Of watching your expertise get reduced to a Perplexity prompt.

"The worst part?" Rachel continued. "AI could generate 50 pitch variations while I was still crafting the perfect subject line. It could build media lists instantly. It knew which journalists covered what beats. Everything I'd built my agency on, AI could do faster and cheaper."

Then came the twist: Journalists started posting that they'd automatically reject any pitch that felt AI-generated.

"So, I couldn't use AI without feeling like I would be blacklisted, but my competitors who were using it smartly were producing content at ten times my speed," Rachel said. "I felt trapped between becoming a dinosaur or becoming inauthentic."

The Client Reality Check

Rachel's biggest client dropped the bomb during a routine check-in: "Rachel, I can use ChatGPT to write press releases too. So why exactly am I paying you?"

Ouch. But that honesty became an important moment in her business pivot.

"I realized AI could write ABOUT my clients, but it couldn't KNOW them," Rachel explained. "It couldn't sit in their conference room and sense the unspoken dynamics. It couldn't catch the CEO's hesitation when discussing company values and dig deeper. It couldn't help a nervous founder push past their fear of being vulnerable to share the story that would connect with people. It couldn't hear the subtle excitement when they mentioned a small detail they thought was insignificant but was the heart of everything. It couldn't recognize when someone was playing it safe and encourage them to dream bigger, to own their vision instead of diluting it. AI could find data and statistics, but it couldn't find the human story that was hiding in plain sight—the one the client didn't even know they had."

That's when Rachel stopped seeing AI as her replacement and started seeing it as her research assistant. But the journey wasn't smooth. It required a lot of trial and error.

Rachel's AI Transformation: From Basic to Brilliant

"The game-changer was realizing AI is only as smart as what you teach it," Rachel explained. "I spent weeks training it on each client's voice, their origin story, their values, what makes them different from every other company saying the same things. I fed it their founder's backgrounds, their company culture, even their inside jokes."

Now Rachel's approach is sophisticated. She prompts AI: "You are trained on [Client Name]'s brand voice, values of [list values], and key differentiators including [unique aspects]. Generate 10 creative pitch angles for their [announcement/news] that would appeal to business journalists who typically cover underdogs disrupting traditional industries. Focus on human interest angles that haven't been overdone."

But here's where it gets interesting—she uses AI as her creative partner. Her prompt: "Based on [Client]'s background in [industry] and their mission to [goal], ask me 5 probing questions that might uncover story angles I haven't considered. Think like a journalist looking for exclusive angles."

The AI might respond with questions like: "Has the founder's previous failure in this space informed their current approach?"

or "What would their biggest competitor say about their innovation?" These questions spark conversations with clients that uncover gold.

Rachel's Predictive PR Strategy

Rachel's real innovation? Predictive pitching. Predictive pitching means anticipating what journalists will want to cover before they even know they want it. Instead of pitching stories when everyone else is and competing for attention, Rachel positions her clients to be ready with the perfect story right when journalists start looking for that exact angle. It's like knowing winter is coming and having coats ready to sell instead of trying to push beach umbrellas.

An example predictive prompt to AI: "Analyze news cycles and trending topics in [industry]. Based on seasonal patterns and current events, predict what stories [Publication] will be looking for in 30-60 days. Match these predictions with [Client]'s potential news hooks."

"I'm not pitching today's news anymore," Rachel said. "I'm positioning clients for next month's trends. When everyone else is reactive, we're proactive."

The Art of Prompt Engineering

Prompt engineering sounds fancy but basically means learning how to talk to AI so it doesn't give you responses that sound like they were written by a robot having an existential crisis. It's the difference between asking AI "write about my client" (yawn) and giving it the context, personality, and strategic direction that creates magic.

Rachel learned the hard way that generic prompts get generic results. Now she uses prompts like:

"Acting as a PR strategist who understands Entrepreneur magazine loves stories about founders who risked everything to solve personal problems that became million-dollar businesses, create 5 pitch angles for [Client]'s Series A announcement. Context: Founder quit her Fortune 500 exec job, cashed out her 401k, and lived on ramen for two years to solve [specific problem] that frustrated her daily. The solution now helps 50,000 customers who had the same problem. Focus on: personal sacrifice, relatable problems that others experience, journey from corporate comfort to startup struggle, and specific moment she knew she had to build this."

"The prompt engineering is everything," Rachel emphasized. "Garbage in, garbage out. But strategic context in? Magic out."

Strategic PR That Actually Drives Revenue

"The biggest shift in my business wasn't just using AI—it was linking every piece of press to actual business outcomes," Rachel explained. "I stopped counting media hits and started measuring revenue impact."

Rachel now uses AI to ensure strategic placement. Her prompt: "Analyze [Client]'s ideal customer profile: [demographics, pain points, buying behavior]. Match this with the readership/listenership data of these media outlets: [list]. Rank opportunities by likelihood to reach actual buyers, not just generate impressions. Include podcasts where their target audience actively listens, speaking opportunities at conferences where buyers gather, and awards that their customers actually care about."

"My clients used to get excited about any press mention," Rachel said. "Now we're strategic. That startup might have gotten into 25 small publications before, but one feature in the specific trade magazine their buyers read drives more sales than all 25 mentions combined."

She shared an example: "I had a B2B software client who kept wanting TechCrunch coverage. But their buyers—HR directors at mid-size companies—don't read TechCrunch. They read HR Executive magazine and listen to specific HR podcasts during their commutes. We pivoted the entire strategy. Less sexy on paper, but their sales increased."

Rachel's new mantra: "I don't measure success by the size of the publication anymore. I measure it by whether my client's ideal customer saw it and took action. Quality over quantity, strategy over vanity metrics."

"I'm not a publicist anymore," Rachel said. "I'm a revenue-driving strategic partner who uses PR as the vehicle. My clients don't hire me for press releases—they hire me for business growth through strategic visibility."

Her new pricing model? "I charge based on strategic value, not hours spent writing.

She Leads as a CEO & Business Owner

💭 TAKE A PAUSE, FRIEND

Before diving into strategies, let's reflect honestly about your current business reality:

1. **When was your last actual day off?** Not "working from my phone at the beach" but OFF? If you can't remember, we have work to do.

2. **What percentage of your day is spent on visionary CEO work versus tasks a smart assistant could handle?** Be honest—are you the CEO or the chief everything officer?

3. **The sick test:** If you got the flu tomorrow (heaven forbid), how many hours could your business survive without you? Hours? Days? Minutes?

4. **What's one big dream for your business you've shelved** because you're too busy putting out daily fires?

5. **Are you building a business or just a really demanding job** with no boss to blame but yourself?

CEO AI Strategies That Actually Work

Here are practical strategies that transform overwhelmed CEOs into actual leaders:

1. **The "Not Everything Needs Me" Decision System**
   Stop being the bottleneck in your own business.

   Implementation prompt: "Here's a list of all decisions made in my business daily: [list them]. Create a decision matrix showing: 1) Decisions only the CEO should make (vision, major partnerships, values), 2) Decisions needing input but not execution, 3) Decisions to automate or delegate. Include specific criteria and examples for each category."

Example: Melanie's consulting firm was drowning in micro-decisions. Now AI handles: project assignments under $50K, standard contract modifications, routine client communications. She focuses on strategic partnerships and innovation. "I make 10 important decisions weekly instead of 100 unimportant ones daily."

2. **The Client Experience Automation (That Still Feels Personal)** Deliver exceptional experiences without personally managing every touchpoint.

   Implementation prompt: "Here's my client journey: [list each step from inquiry to completion]. For each touchpoint, identify: 1) Where CEO involvement adds irreplaceable value, 2) Where AI can create personalized communications maintaining my voice, 3) Specific templates needed. Create 5 sample templates based on my writing style: [paste 2-3 examples of your emails]."

   Example: Business coach Julie mapped her 12-touchpoint client journey, then created AI templates for each. Her prompt for welcome emails: "Using my writing style from the examples provided, welcome new client [name] to our program. Reference their specific goal of [goal from intake form], acknowledge their biggest challenge of [challenge], and share excitement about their journey. Tone: warm, professional, personally invested but not overly formal. Include next steps and calendar link. Sign off the way I typically do."

Result: Clients feel personally welcomed while Julie focuses on high-value coaching. "They often tell me how thoughtful my emails are," she laughed. "AI helps me be thoughtful at scale."

3. **The "Show Me What Matters" Financial Dashboard** Transform your financial reports from overwhelming to insightful.

Implementation prompt: "I'm uploading my financial reports: P&L, Cash Flow Statement, and Sales by Product/Service. Analyze these and create a CEO dashboard showing: 1) Current cash position and runway at current burn rate (how many months until we run out of money at current spending), 2) Top 3 revenue sources with growth trends, 3) Any expense categories growing faster than revenue, 4) One actionable insight I should address this week. Skip everything that's fine—only show what needs attention."

Example: Jennifer, a marketing consultant, exported her financial reports monthly for AI analysis. "I discovered Service 1 that I was pushing hard had 5% margins, while Service 2 that I barely promoted had 40% margins. My financial software showed me all the numbers, but AI showed me what the numbers meant. I was focusing on all the wrong things because I was buried in data instead of insights."

Pro tip: Set up a monthly ritual: export financial reports → AI analysis. Takes 15 minutes, saves hours of spreadsheet staring, and tells you what to do next.

4. **The Strategic Content System** Maintain thought leadership without living at your keyboard.

   Implementation prompt: "I'm recording 15 minutes on [topic]. Transform into: 1) Blog post maintaining my stories and speech patterns, 2) 5 social posts that sound conversational, not corporate, 3) Email newsletter with my personality intact. Include my favorite phrases: [list them]."

   Pro tip: Monthly "brain dump" sessions where you talk to your phone about what's on your heart. AI transforms it into content that sounds like you, not a LinkedIn robot trying to sound professional.

5. **The Energy Protection Protocol** Build a business that energizes instead of exhausts.

   Implementation prompt: "Here's my calendar for the past month with my energy notes: [list activities marked as energizing vs draining]. Based on this pattern, analyze: 1) What types of activities consistently energize me, 2) What tasks drain me unnecessarily, 3) When do I have peak energy during the day, 4) How can I restructure my schedule to protect my energy for CEO work. Be specific about what to move, delegate, or delete."

   Example: Designer Ashley tracked her energy for two weeks, marking each calendar item as energizing, neutral, or draining. Her AI analysis revealed she scheduled creative work post-lunch (her lowest energy) and admin during mornings (her peak). She also discovered client strategy sessions energized her while project status meetings drained her. She flipped her schedule to do creative work in the mornings. She was working the same hours but doubled her output with half the exhaustion.

Pro tip: Spend one week adding simple energy notes to your calendar (E for energizing, D for draining). The patterns AI finds will surprise you.

Advanced CEO Strategies (When You're Ready to Level Up)

Ready to scale like a true visionary? Here's next-level implementation:

1. **The Market Intelligence System** Stay ahead without the obsession.

   Advanced prompt: "Here's my business: [describe your services, ideal clients, and unique value proposition]. My top 3 competitors are: [list them]. Create a monthly competitive intelligence brief (one page max) showing: 1) Major moves by these competitors that could impact my business, 2) Market opportunities they're missing that align with my strengths, 3) One bold strategic move I could make based on market gaps. Search current industry trends in [your industry] and skip the noise—only show actionable intelligence."

2. **The Scale-Without-Stress Architecture** Build systems for growth without growing your to-do list.

Advanced prompt: "Here are my core business processes: [list your main processes like client onboarding, service delivery, invoicing, etc.]. For each process, analyze: 1) Current state with steps involved, 2) What this process needs to look like at 10x current volume, 3) Specific changes needed including what to automate, what to delegate to team members, and what to eliminate. Create a priority list for implementation based on impact and ease. Be realistic about timeline and resources needed."

3. **The Strategic Partnership Multiplier** Find partnerships that multiply impact, not tasks.

    Advanced prompt: "My business serves [describe ideal client] with [your services]. My strengths are [list them] and my gaps are [list them]. Research and identify 5 potential strategic partners who: 1) Serve my ideal clients with complementary services, 2) Have strengths where I have gaps, 3) Share similar values based on their public content and messaging. For each partner, suggest creative collaboration structures like: joint programs, bundled services, cross-referrals with incentives, co-created content, or shared events. Go beyond basic referral agreements."

4. **The Innovation Pipeline** Stay innovative without innovation exhaustion.

    Advanced prompt: "Create an innovation evaluation system for my [type of business]. Include: 1) Five yes/no questions to quickly assess if an opportunity aligns with my business goals, 2) A simple testing protocol that requires less than [X hours] and [$X budget] to validate ideas, 3) Clear go/no-go criteria based on results, 4) A 'parking lot' system for good ideas that aren't right timing. Make this a framework I can use in 15 minutes or less to evaluate any new opportunity."

Real-World CEO Transformations That Inspire

Patricia's Freedom Story: Built AI-powered assessment tools for her HR consulting firm by training AI on her diagnostic methods and frameworks. Her team now delivers expert-level consulting without direct involvement.

Nina's Creative Scale: Trained AI on her design principles, color preferences, and style guidelines. Created a system where her team inputs client requirements and AI generates initial concepts in her signature style. She approves and refines while her team handles production.

Denise's Coaching Revolution: Systematized her coaching methodology into AI-supported workflows. AI handles intake questionnaires, sends personalized check-ins between sessions, tracks client progress, and suggests session focus areas. She now serves 50 clients with deeper impact than when she served 10.

DO THIS NOW, NOT LATER

Pick ONE action to reclaim your CEO role this week:

Action 1: The Unfiltered Time Truth Track everything for three days. Prompt AI: "Analyze this time log. Show: 1) Percentage of actual CEO work, 2) Tasks I do from habit not necessity, 3) The ONE thing to stop immediately for maximum time recovery. Don't sugarcoat it.

Action 2: The Revenue Reality Check Prompt: "Analyze revenue and time data. Calculate profit per hour for each service/product. What should I double down on? What should I kill? Don't spare my feelings—show me the truth."

Action 3: The Task Freedom System Choose your most annoying daily task. Build a complete system this week. Not someday. This week.

Action 4: The Sacred CEO Day Block one full day this month for strategic thinking. Out of office on. Let AI handle routine operations. Watch what happens when you lead instead of just labor.

A COACH'S NOTE ✉

Friend, I see you. Checking email during family dinner. Taking "quick calls" during vacation. Telling yourself "just this quarter" for the tenth quarter in a row.

Here's the permission slip you didn't ask for but desperately need: You're allowed to be a CEO who has boundaries. Who builds systems instead of doing everything. Who works on vision while operations run smoothly.

Your business isn't your baby that needs 24/7 attention, it's a vehicle for your vision that should run well with a good driver, not an exhausted one.

The guilt you feel about delegating, that's not wisdom, it's conditioning. The fear that things will fall apart without you, that's not intuition, it's a sign you haven't built the right systems yet.

Start with one system. Delegate one decision. Protect one hour. Your future self, the one enjoying her success instead of drowning in it, will thank you.

Remember: The goal was never to build a prison with a company logo. The goal was freedom, impact, and a life you love.

CHAPTER 17 QUICK REFERENCE

Key Mindset Shifts:

- You're the CEO, not the Chief Everything Officer
- Systems scale your thinking, not your stress
- A business needing you 24/7 isn't successful, it's unsustainable
- Vision drives value, not task completion

CEO AI Strategies:

- Not Everything Needs Me Decision System—delegate with confidence
- Client Experience Automation—exceptional service without personal overwhelm
- Show Me What Matters Dashboard—insights over information
- Strategic Content System—thought leadership in 1/10th the time
- Energy Protection Protocol—build a business that energizes you

Advanced Strategies:

- Market Intelligence System—stay ahead without obsession
- Scale-Without-Stress Architecture—grow impact, not hours

- Strategic Partnership Multiplier—collaborate for exponential growth
- Innovation Pipeline—stay fresh without burnout

Your Action Step: Choose ONE task you do daily that doesn't require CEO thinking. Create a system this week. Start your freedom.

Remember: Your business should serve your life, not consume it.

> You didn't start your business to become its servant. You started it to create freedom, impact, and meaning. AI helps you reclaim all three.
>
> — T. RENEÉ SMITH

PART IV

YOUR AI-POWERED FUTURE

> *"You're not just adapting to the future—you're creating it."*
>
> *– T. Reneé Smith*

Here we are, beautiful soul. What a journey we've been on together. You've discovered that AI isn't your competition, it's your collaboration partner, here to amplify everything that makes you irreplaceable. You've given yourself permission to accept support without guilt and redefined success to include both achievement and peace. You've explored how AI can enhance every aspect of who you are as a woman—your spirituality, your health, your relationships, and your inner world. You've seen how AI supports you in every role you play—as a wife, mother, daughter, sister, friend, and professional leader.

Now comes the part I'm most excited about: **building your strategic roadmap for an AI-enhanced life.**

This isn't about adding more complexity to your already full plate. This is about creating a clear strategy that honors your values while leveraging technology's power. This is about understanding that you're not just learning to use AI—you're learning to lead with it.

What You'll Discover in This Section:

Chapter 18: Your AI Personal Strategic Roadmap You'll master the **T.I.M.E. Human-Centered AI™ Strategy Framework** — your personal blueprint for AI success that works with any tool, in any season, for any goal. No more overwhelm from endless options. Just clear strategy for building an AI ecosystem that serves your unique life without consuming it.

Chapter 19: Leading Your Organization's AI Transformation You'll master the **G.U.I.D.E. Framework for Human-Centered AI™ Transformation** - a proven approach for leaders who want to put people first. You'll discover how to navigate resistance, build enthusiasm, and create AI transformation that amplifies your team's capabilities rather than diminishing their value.

Chapter 20: History-Makers: Your Role in the AI Revolution Discover why women are uniquely positioned to shape the AI future and how to claim your seat at the table where decisions are being made

Chapter 21: The Movement She Leads and She Loves™ You'll discover the power of doing this journey in community. The She Leads and She Loves™ movement isn't just about individual success—it's about collective transformation. Because when women support each other in embracing AI strategically, we all rise.

Most importantly, you'll understand that your AI journey isn't just about personal efficiency, it's about modeling a new way of living and leading in the digital age. You're part of a movement of women proving that embracing AI doesn't mean sacrificing what makes us human. Instead, it means having more capacity to focus on what matters most.

You're not just becoming AI-empowered. You're becoming a leader in the most important conversation of our time: what it means to be fully human in an age of artificial intelligence.

The future belongs to women like you—women who can hold both technological intelligence and emotional wisdom, strategic thinking and compassionate action, efficient systems and authentic relationships. Women who understand that the question isn't whether to embrace AI, but how to embrace it in a way that amplifies rather than diminishes our humanity.

That future doesn't require you to master every new tool that launches. It requires you to master the strategy of knowing what serves your vision and what's just digital noise.

That future starts now, sis. And it starts with strategy, not tools.

CHAPTER 18

YOUR PERSONAL AI STRATEGIC ROADMAP: FROM OVERWHELM TO OWNERSHIP

> "Tools without strategy is just digital clutter. Strategy without tools is just wishful thinking."
>
> – T. Reneé Smith

When Research Almost Broke My Brain (And Why That's Good News for You)

Y'all, let me tell you about the time I almost lost my mind trying to become an AI expert for this book.

Picture this: I had 25 browser tabs open (I counted), was following 13 different AI "gurus" on social media and had signed up for so many AI newsletters that my inbox looked like it had been attacked by robots. I was four weeks into my research phase, and instead of feeling informed, I felt like my brain was being held hostage by acronyms—GPT, LLM, NLP, API... Lord help me.

One morning, I found myself watching a tutorial about creating an AI avatar that was supposed to look and sound exactly like me. Two hours later, I had a digital clone that looked like me if I'd been animated by someone who'd never actually seen a human face. The lip sync? Let's just say it looked like I was dubbing a kung fu movie. Badly.

That's when my teenager walked by, took one look at my screen, and said, "Mom, what is that supposed to be?"

"It's my AI avatar," I said, trying to sound confident.

He tilted his head. "It looks like you're having an allergic reaction while speaking a different language."

He wasn't wrong.

But here's the thing—I'm persistent. So, I spent another few hours learning the platform, adjusting settings, tweaking the voice modulation, and figuring out lighting angles I didn't even know mattered. By the next day, that avatar looked so much like me it was almost creepy (in a good way). The voice? After some fine-tuning, my own mother couldn't tell the difference.

The lesson? The tools are incredible—when you have time to master them. But who has days to perfect an avatar when you've got a business to run, a family to feed, and a life to live?

That night, I had a revelation while sipping my hot tea. I asked myself a question: If I—someone who genuinely loves research and considers learning new technology fun—was this overwhelmed, what about the women who just want AI to help them get dinner on the table without spending three hours cooking?

That's when I decided to become your sacrificial lamb. I would test different tools, follow as many gurus as I could find, and try every ridiculous AI experiment (yes, including the one where AI was supposed to plan my entire wardrobe but kept suggesting I dress half my age). I would wade through the chaos, so you don't have to.

Consider this chapter my gift to you: Everything I learned from nearly pulling my hair out, distilled into what matters for real women with real lives. No acronyms required. No avatar mastery necessary (unless you want one—then I'll tell you exactly which platform works). Just practical tools that solve actual problems without requiring a computer science degree or weeks of trial and error.

Because here's what I discovered after testing approximately 837 AI tools (slight exaggeration, but not by much): You don't need to master them all, you need a strategic framework that works with any tool. Not a collection of random apps. Not endless subscriptions you'll forget about. A strategy.

So put down the 19 AI apps you downloaded last week and never opened. Close those 47 browser tabs about "revolutionary AI tools that will change everything." And definitely don't spend four days perfecting an avatar unless that's genuinely going to transform your business (spoiler: for most of us, it won't).

What you need is a way to evaluate, integrate, and evolve your AI approach as new tools emerge—because they will, constantly. That's exactly what this chapter delivers.

Let's talk about what works.

Strategy First, Tools Second

After my avatar adventure and research spiral, I had an epiphany. I was collecting AI tools like they were designer handbags—grabbing whatever looked good without asking if they matched the outfits I already had in my closet. No wonder my brain was scattered. I had tools for problems I didn't even have while my real challenges went unaddressed.

That's when it hit me. Throughout this book, I've given you specific prompts for everything from meal planning to business strategy. You've learned how AI can support your faith, health, relationships, and leadership. But what you really need isn't another tool recommendation—you need a strategic framework for bringing it all together.

New AI tools launch literally every day. By the time this book is in your hands, there will be innovations I couldn't have imagined while writing it. But strategy? Strategy is timeless.

That's why this chapter isn't about tools, it's about building your personal AI roadmap that works with any tool, in any season of life, for any goal you're pursuing.

T.I.M.E Human-Centered AI™ Strategy Framework: Your Strategic Foundation

This framework isn't just for choosing tools, it's for strategically integrating AI into every decision about how technology serves your life:

T	Target Your True Needs	Not what's trendy, but what truly needs transformation in your life
I	Integrate With Intention	Not random implementation, but purposeful integration that honors your values
M	Measure What Matters	Not vanity metrics, but meaningful measures of life improvement
E	Evolve Your Ecosystem	Not one-and-done, but continuous evolution as your life changes

Your Three Strategic Spheres

As you build your AI roadmap, think in three interconnected spheres:

- **Sphere 1: Personal Mastery** This is your foundation—health, spirituality, finances, self-care, personal growth. When this sphere is strong, everything else flows better.
- **Sphere 2: Professional Impact** This is your contribution—career, business, leadership, expertise. Where you multiply your gifts to serve others.
- **Sphere 3: Life Architecture** This is your infrastructure—systems, schedules, household, coordination. The invisible framework that holds everything together.

The magic happens when these spheres work together, each one strengthening the others.

Building Your Strategic Roadmap Using T.I.M.E Human-Centered AI™ Strategy Framework

Now that you have an overview of the TIME framework, let's walk through it together, step by step. This is your personal workbook section—grab a notebook and work through each element.

Target Your True Needs

Step 1: Assess Your Three Life Spheres

Rate your current satisfaction in each sphere (1-10). *(1 = constant stress/crisis, 5 = managing but exhausting, 10 = flowing smoothly with ease)*:

Personal Mastery Sphere

- Health & Wellness: ___/10
- Spiritual Practice: ___/10
- Financial Wellness: ___/10
- Self-Care & Joy: ___/10
- Personal Growth: ___/10

Professional Impact Sphere

- Career or Business Satisfaction: ___/10
- Leadership Effectiveness: ___/10
- Work-Life Integration: ___/10
- Professional Growth: ___/10
- Impact & Contribution: ___/10

Life Architecture Sphere

- Home Organization: ___/10
- Schedule Management: ___/10
- Family Coordination: ___/10
- Meal Planning: ___/10
- Administrative Tasks: ___/10

Step 2: Identify Your Primary Pain Point

Look at your lowest scores. Which ONE issue, if solved, would create the biggest positive ripple effect in your life?

Write it here:

_____

This becomes your starting point. Be specific:

- Vague example: "I need better work-life balance"
- Measurable example: "I spend 10 hours weekly on email management that drains my energy"

I - Integrate With Intention

Step 3: Design Your Integration Plan

Based on your primary pain point, answer these questions:

What does success look like? (Be specific: "I want to reduce email time to 3 hours weekly and use the saved 7 hours for strategic thinking")

What's my learning style? ❐ Jump in and figure it out ❐ Step-by-step guidance needed ❐ Learn with others/accountability

When will I practice? ❐ Morning (5-7 AM) ❐ Lunch break ❐ Evening (8-10 PM) ❐ Weekend blocks

What could derail me? (List your typical obstacles: perfectionism, comparison, lack of time, etc.)

Write it here:

_____

Step 4: Choose Your First AI Application

Based on your pain point, select ONE AI tool or application to start with. Don't research 20 options—pick one that addresses your specific challenge and commit to it for 30 days.

AI Prompt to Find Your Tool: "I need an AI tool to help with [insert your specific pain point]. My budget is [free/under $20/month/flexible]. I'm a [beginner/intermediate/advanced] tech user. I need something I can learn in less than an hour and use daily. What are the top 2-3 options, and which would you recommend starting with?"

M - Measure What Matters

Step 5: Define Your Success Metrics

Create both quantitative and qualitative measures:

Quantitative Metrics (measurable):

- Time saved per week: _____
  (Example: From 10 hours on email to 3 hours = 7 hours save")

- Tasks automated: _____
  (Example: 5 weekly reports now auto-generated)

- Money saved: _____
  (Example:$200/month not hiring VA for these task)

- Stress level (1-10) before: _____ Goal: _____ *(Example: Before: 8, Goal: 4)*

- Other: _____

Qualitative Metrics (feeling-based):

- Energy at end of day: _____
  (Example: Energized enough to cook dinner vs. ordering takeout)
- Presence with family: _____
  (Example: Actually listening at dinner vs. mentally at work)
- Joy in work: _____
  (Example: Excited about projects vs. dreading Mondays)
- Overall life satisfaction: _____
  (Example: Feel like I'm thriving vs. just surviving)

Step 6: Create Your Tracking System

Choose your method: ☐ Daily journal (2 minutes before bed) ☐ Weekly check-in (Sunday planning) ☐ Phone notes throughout the day ☐ Accountability partner check-ins

E - Evolve Your Ecosystem

Step 7: Plan Your Evolution Path

Month 1-2: Foundation

- Master your ONE chosen AI application
- Track your metrics weekly
- Celebrate small wins
- Don't add anything new yet

Month 3-4: Enhancement

- Optimize what's working: Double down on features saving you the most time

- Explore advanced features: Try automation rules or integrations you skipped initially

- Create templates/shortcuts: Save your best prompts and workflows for reuse

- Consider a complementary tool: Add one that works with your first tool (like note-taking AI + meeting recorder, or meal planning AI + grocery delivery automation)

Month 5-6: Expansion

- Choose a second pain point in the SAME sphere: Personal Mastery, Professional Impact or Life Architecture

- Apply what you've learned: Use the same implementation process (assess, choose tool, track metrics) but move 2x faster with your experience

- Begin connecting tools if beneficial: Look for ways your AI tools can share information or trigger each other (example: one tool's output becomes another tool's input)

- Document your systems: write down what works so you can replicate and teach others

Month 6+: Elevation

- Expand to a second sphere: select the next sphere that needs your attention (Personal Mastery, Professional Impact or Life Architecture)

- Create interconnected systems: build workflows where tools from different spheres work together, turning isolated tasks into connected processes
- Share your success with others: teach a friend, post in the community, or mentor someone starting out
- Continuously refine: monthly check-ins to adjust as your life evolves

Your T.I.M.E Human-Centered AI™ Strategy Framework Implementation Worksheet

Fill this out now:

T - My biggest pain point is:

_____

I - I will integrate AI by:

- Practicing at: _____ (time)
- For: _____ minutes daily
- Using: _____ (tool/application)

M - I will measure success by:

- Quantitative: _____
- Qualitative: _____

E - My 30-day commitment:

"I commit to using _____ for _____ every day for 30 days before evaluating or adding anything new."

Signature: _____   Date: _____

💬 TAKE A PAUSE, FRIEND: QUICK REALITY CHECK

Before you start:

1. Is your pain point specific enough to measure improvement? ☐ Yes ☐ No
2. Have you chosen just ONE tool to start? ☐ Yes ☐ No
3. Are your success metrics realistic for 30 days? ☐ Yes ☐ No
4. Do you have accountability in place? ☐ Yes ☐ No

If you answered "no" to any of these, go back and refine before starting.

The 7-Day Quick Start

- ✓ **Day 1:** Complete the TIME worksheet
- ✓ **Day 2:** Set up your chosen AI tool
- ✓ **Day 3:** Use it for your specific pain point
- ✓ **Day 4:** Track your first results
- ✓ **Day 5:** Adjust based on what you learned
- ✓ **Day 6:** Establish a routine
- ✓ **Day 7:** Celebrate and plan week 2

Strategic Decision Framework

For every AI opportunity that comes your way after your initial success, ask:

1. **Alignment Check** Does this serve my strategic vision or is it just shiny?
   - Aligned with current phase (Step 1 – Step 6)? Proceed.
   - Interesting but off-strategy? Save for later.
   - Completely unrelated? Let it go.

2. **Capacity Assessment** Do I have bandwidth to implement this well?
   - Mental capacity to learn?
   - Time capacity to implement?
   - Emotional capacity for temporary frustration?

3. **Integration Evaluation** Will this strengthen or complicate my ecosystem?
   - Enhances existing systems? Green light.
   - Requires starting over? Yellow light.
   - Creates more complexity? Red light.

4. **Value Verification** Is the benefit worth the investment?
   - Clear ROI on time/energy? Yes.
   - Marginal improvement? Maybe.
   - Effort exceeds benefit? No.

Your Living Roadmap

Your AI strategy isn't static—it's a living document that evolves with you:

Quarterly Reviews

- What's working brilliantly?
- What needs adjustment?
- What new opportunities have emerged?
- How have my priorities shifted?

Annual Vision Refresh

- How has AI transformation impacted my life?
- What new possibilities do I see?
- Where do I want to grow next?
- How can I serve others with what I've learned?

Strategic Wisdom from the Journey

After guiding hundreds of women through AI transformation, here's what I know:

Start Where It Hurts Most: The biggest pain point provides the highest motivation to persist through the learning curve.

Progress Over Perfection: A 50% improvement you implement beats a 100% solution you never start.

Community Accelerates Everything: That's why She Leads and She Loves™ exists—to share real strategies, real tools, and real support as the landscape evolves.

Your Humanity Is Your Differentiator: AI handles the mechanical so you can focus on the meaningful.

DO THIS NOW, NOT LATER

Action 1: Complete Your T.I.M.E Human-Centered AI™ Strategy Framework Don't just read this chapter—work through it. Fill out every section of the Implementation Worksheet. This is your strategic foundation.

Action 2: Choose Your Starting Point Based on your assessment, pick your ONE pain point and ONE tool. Write them down. Make them real.

Action 3: Set Your Start Date Put Day 1 of your 7-day quick start on your calendar. Not "someday." An actual date within the next 7 days.

Action 4: Find Your Accountability Text one friend about your AI journey. Share your pain point and your 30-day commitment. Ask them to check in weekly.

A COACH'S NOTE 💌

Friend, as you close this chapter, you might feel the tension between excitement and overwhelm. You see the possibilities, but you also see the journey ahead.

Here's what I want you to remember: You don't have to have it all figured out. You just need to know your next right step.

Throughout this book, you've learned specific applications and prompts. You've seen how AI can serve every area of your life. Now you have the strategic framework to bring it all together in a way that makes sense for YOUR life.

The beauty of the **T.I.M.E Human-Centered AI™ Strategy Framework** is that it grows with you. As new tools emerge, as your life evolves, as your priorities shift—your strategy adapts while your foundation remains strong.

You're not behind. You're not too late. You're exactly where you need to be—equipped with both practical knowledge and strategic wisdom to build an AI-enhanced life that honors everything you hold dear.

Trust your instincts. Start where it matters most. Build steadily. And remember—we're doing this together.

CHAPTER 18 QUICK REFERENCE

The T.I.M.E Human-Centered AI™ Strategy Framework:

- Target your true needs
- Integrate with intention

- Measure what matters
- Evolve your ecosystem

Three Strategic Spheres:

- Personal Mastery: Health, spirituality, finances, self-care
- Professional Impact: Career, business, leadership
- Life Architecture: Systems, schedules, coordination

Your 7-Day Quick Start:

- Day 1: Complete TIME worksheet
- Day 2: Set up chosen tool
- Day 3-7: Implement, track, adjust

Your Action Step: Complete your **T.I.M.E Human-Centered AI™ Strategy Framework** implementation worksheet TODAY.

Remember: The framework isn't just theory—it's your practical roadmap to AI success.

> New tools launch daily, but strategy is timeless. Build your roadmap once, adapt it forever.
>
> —T. Reneé Smith

CHAPTER 19

LEADING YOUR ORGANIZATION'S AI TRANSFORMATION

> *"Leadership in the AI age means transforming fear into opportunity, resistance into readiness."*
> – T. Reneé Smith

The CEO Who Almost Started an Office Uprising

I'll never forget the panic in Patricia's voice when she called me. "T. Reneé, I think I just made a huge mistake," she said. Patricia was the CEO of a mid-sized financial services firm, and earlier that day, she'd announced their new "AI-First Initiative" at an all-hands meeting.

"The room went cold," she told me. "I could literally see people's faces shut down. One of my best managers asked point-blank if they should start updating their resumes". Another said,

"Great, one more thing to learn on top of everything else." Patricia thought she was inspiring them, but she was invoking fear about job stability without realizing it.

Patricia had done what so many well-meaning leaders do, she'd focused on the technology without considering the humans who'd need to embrace it. She'd talked about efficiency gains and competitive advantages while her team heard "You're replaceable" and "Your job is changing whether you like it or not."

"How do I fix this?" she asked.

That conversation led to a six-month transformation that not only successfully integrated AI across her organization but increased employee engagement and retention. The secret? We didn't start with the technology. We started with the people.

By the time we were done, her employees were coming to HER with AI ideas. The same manager who'd asked about updating his resume? He became their AI champion, leading training sessions and mentoring others.

The difference? Patricia learned to lead AI transformation with our **G.U.I.D.E. Framework for Human-Centered AI™ Transformation** —an approach that puts people at the center of technological change.

Why Most AI Initiatives Fail (And How Yours Won't)

70% of organizational AI initiatives fail. Not because the technology doesn't work, but because leaders forget that organizations are made of people, not processes.

Here's what typically happens:

- Leadership gets excited about AI's potential (usually after a conference or competitor announcement)

- They announce a big AI initiative with lots of buzzwords
- Employees hear "layoffs coming" regardless of what's said
- Resistance builds, adoption stalls, and the initiative dies a slow, expensive death
- Everyone concludes "AI doesn't work for us"

But here's the truth: AI transformation isn't a technology challenge—it's a leadership challenge. And if you're reading this book, you already have everything you need to lead it successfully.

The G.U.I.D.E. Framework for Human-Centered AI™ Transformation: Your Organizational AI Strategy

After working with dozens of organizations, I've developed the G.U.I.D.E. framework for AI transformation that works:

G	Gauge Organizational Readiness	Not just technical readiness, but human readiness
U	Unite Leadership and Vision	Create aligned, authentic messaging that inspires rather than terrifies
I	Identify Strategic Opportunities	Find where AI amplifies human capability and creates new possibilities
D	Develop Your People First	Build confidence and capability before deploying technology
E	Execute with Empathy	Roll out with care, celebrate wins, and adjust based on feedback

Let's break this down into actionable strategy:

G - Gauge Organizational Readiness

Before you mention AI in any company communication, assess three critical areas:

Technical Readiness:

- Current technology infrastructure
- Data quality and accessibility
- Security and compliance capabilities
- Integration possibilities

Cultural Readiness:

- Current comfort with change
- Learning culture strength
- Trust levels between leadership and teams
- Past technology adoption experiences

Human Readiness:

- Skill gaps and learning capacity
- Change fatigue levels
- Job security concerns
- Innovation appetite

Patricia's mistake? She assessed technical readiness (strong) but ignored human readiness (terrified). Don't make the same error.

💬 TAKE A PAUSE, LEADER: YOUR READINESS REALITY CHECK

Get honest about where your organization really stands:

Technical Questions:

1. Can your current systems handle AI integration, or are you building on shaky foundations?
2. Is your data organized enough for AI to use it effectively?
3. Do you have basic security measures in place to use AI responsibly?

Cultural Questions:

1. When you announced the last major change, how did people really react? (Not what they said in meetings, but what they said when you weren't around)
2. Do people generally trust that leadership has their best interests at heart?
3. How much change has your team absorbed in the last 18 months?

Human Questions:

1. What percentage of your team is genuinely excited about learning new technologies?
2. How many people are worried about job security right now?
3. Who are your potential AI champions hiding in plain sight?

U - Unite Leadership and Vision

Here's where Patricia turned things around. Instead of top-down mandates, we created a unified vision that addressed what people cared about:

The Vision Reframe:

- FROM: "AI will make us more efficient"
- TO: "AI will free you to do work that matters more"
- FROM: "We need to stay competitive"
- TO: "We're investing in tools that invest in you"
- FROM: "This transformation is critical"
- TO: "We're going to learn and grow together"

Creating Your AI Vision Statement:

1. Acknowledge current challenges people face
2. Paint a picture of AI solving those specific problems
3. Emphasize human value and growth
4. Include everyone in the journey
5. Be specific about what won't change

Patricia's revised vision: "We're bringing in AI to handle the repetitive tasks that steal your time and energy, so you can focus on the strategic thinking and relationship building that made you choose this career. Your expertise becomes more valuable, not less, when AI handles the mundane."

I - Identify Strategic Opportunities

Focus on identifying where AI can elevate your team's performance and upskill employees to do work that truly utilizes their expertise and passion.

The Opportunity Matrix: Map opportunities across two dimensions:

1. Human Impact: How much does this free people to do higher-value work?
2. Business Value: How much does this advance strategic objectives?

Focus on High Human Impact + High Business Value first. These become your proof points that AI serves everyone.

Patricia's First Three Wins:

1. **Report Generation:** AI created first drafts of routine reports, giving analysts 10 hours weekly for actual analysis
2. **Customer Service Enhancement:** AI handled routine inquiries, letting service reps focus on complex problem-solving
3. **Meeting Intelligence:** AI summarized meetings and tracked action items, eliminating hours of administrative work

Notice what these have in common? They made employees' lives better while improving business outcomes.

D - Develop Your People First

This is where most organizations get it backwards. They deploy technology then train people. Instead:

The Development Sequence:

1. **Awareness Building:** Help people understand AI's actual capabilities (versus science fiction fears)

2. **Skill Development:** Teach AI interaction skills (how to write effective prompts, when to use AI vs. human judgment, and how to verify AI output) before deploying tools

3. **Confidence Building:** Start with low-risk applications where people can experiment safely

4. **Champion Creation:** Identify and empower early adopters to mentor others

5. **Continuous Learning:** Build ongoing education into the culture

Patricia's Approach:

- Voluntary AI Literacy Lunches where people could ask any question without judgment

- AI Play Days where teams experimented with tools without pressure to produce

- Peer mentoring programs pairing AI-curious employees with early adopters

- Recognition for creative AI applications, not just efficiency gains

The result? When AI tools were deployed, people were excited to use them, not scared of them.

E - Execute with Empathy

Your rollout strategy matters as much as your technology strategy:

The Empathetic Execution Plan:

Phase 1: Pilot with the Willing (Months 1-2)

- Start with volunteer departments
- Over-communicate progress and learnings
- Celebrate small wins publicly
- Address concerns transparently

Phase 2: Expand with Stories (Months 3-4)

- Share peer success stories (not executive mandates)
- Create opt-in opportunities for new departments
- Provide extensive support and patience
- Never shame late adopters

Phase 3: Scale with Support (Months 5-6)

- Roll out to broader organization
- Maintain high-touch support

- Continue celebrating human achievements enabled by AI
- Adjust based on feedback constantly

Phase 4: Sustain with Culture (Ongoing)

- Embed AI literacy into onboarding
- Create innovation time for AI experimentation
- Recognize AI-enabled human achievements
- Keep evolving based on needs

Real Success Metrics That Matter

Track what indicates success:

Human Metrics:

- Employee engagement scores
- Time spent on meaningful work
- Innovation index (new ideas generated)
- Internal mobility (people growing into new roles)
- Retention of high performers

Business Metrics:

- Customer satisfaction improvements
- Revenue per employee

- Time to market for new initiatives
- Quality improvements
- Strategic goal achievement

Cultural Metrics:

- AI tool adoption rates
- Employee-generated AI ideas
- Cross-department collaboration
- Learning participation rates
- Trust in leadership scores

Common Pitfalls and How to Avoid Them

Pitfall 1: The Big Bang Announcement Avoid: Surprising everyone with a massive AI initiative

Instead: Build awareness gradually, starting with leadership modeling

Pitfall 2: The Efficiency Obsession Avoid: Focusing solely on cost reduction and efficiency Instead: Balance efficiency with human development and innovation

Pitfall 3: The Tech-First Approach Avoid: Leading with features and capabilities

Instead: Lead with problems solved and lives improved

Pitfall 4: The Mandated March Avoid: Forcing adoption through policies

Instead: Create pull through value demonstration (show benefits so compelling that people request access rather than resist requirements)

Pitfall 5: The Set-and-Forget Avoid: Treating AI as a one-time implementation

Instead: Build continuous learning and adaptation into your culture

Your 90-Day Quick Start Guide

Days 1-30: Foundation

- Complete organizational readiness assessment
- Align leadership on vision and approach
- Identify 3 high-impact, high-value opportunities
- Begin awareness building with leadership team

Days 31-60: Preparation

- Launch voluntary AI literacy programs
- Identify and prepare pilot departments
- Develop success metrics and feedback systems
- Create communication strategy that emphasizes people

Days 61-90: Launch

- Begin pilot programs with volunteers
- Over-communicate progress and learnings
- Celebrate early wins (however small)
- Adjust based on feedback rapidly

DO THIS NOW, NOT LATER

Action 1: Leadership Alignment Session Schedule 2 hours with your leadership team. Use the **G.U.I.D.E. Framework for Human-Centered AI™ Transformation** to assess readiness and align on approach before any organizational communication.

Action 2: Find Your Champions Identify 5 people in your organization who are naturally curious about technology. Invite them to be part of your AI advisory group.

Action 3: Craft Your Human-Centered Vision Write your AI vision statement that addresses fears and emphasizes human value. Test it with trusted employees before going organization-wide.

Action 4: Start Small Choose one process that consistently stresses your team. Plan a pilot that makes their lives easier. Success here builds momentum for everything else.

A COACH'S NOTE

Courageous leader,

I know the weight you carry, being responsible for your team's success while caring deeply about their wellbeing and future. The pressure to innovate while the fear of disrupting what works. The challenge of leading change when you're still learning yourself.

Here's what I want you to know: Your uncertainty is your strength. Leaders who pretend to have all the AI answers create fear. Leaders who say, "We're going to figure this out together" create trust.

You don't need to be an AI expert to lead AI transformation. You need to be a human who cares about other humans while stewarding organizational success. That combination—strategic thinking plus genuine care is exactly what AI transformation requires.

Patricia's organization didn't succeed because she became technical. They succeeded because she stayed human while embracing technology. She showed that leadership in the AI age isn't about knowing everything, it's about creating conditions where everyone can learn and grow.

Your people are watching. They're taking cues from how you approach this transformation. When you lead with curiosity instead of certainty, with care and strategy, you give them permission to do the same.

The organizations that will thrive aren't the ones with the best AI technology. They're the ones with leaders brave enough to put people at the center of technological change.

That's who you are—a leader who can guide others through change with both wisdom and heart.

CHAPTER 19 QUICK REFERENCE

The G.U.I.D.E. Framework for Human-Centered AI™ Transformation:

- **G**auge organizational readiness (technical, cultural, human)
- **U**nite leadership and vision (human-centered messaging)
- **I**dentify strategic opportunities (amplify people, and create new possibilities)
- **D**evelop your people first (skills before tools)
- **E**xecute with empathy (pilot, expand, scale, sustain)

Success Metrics That Matter:

- Human: Engagement, meaningful work, innovation, growth
- Business: Satisfaction, revenue per employee, quality
- Cultural: Adoption, ideas generated, collaboration, trust

Your Action Step: Schedule your leadership alignment session using the **G.U.I.D.E. Framework for Human-Centered AI™ Transformation** this week

Remember: The best leaders focus on equipping their people with AI capabilities rather than fearing the changes AI brings.

> AI transformation isn't a technology challenge—it's a leadership challenge. When you lead with humanity, your people embrace the journey.
>
> —T. Reneé Smith

CHAPTER 20

WRITING HISTORY-WOMEN WHO LEAD AI TRANSFORMATION

> *"History-makers don't wait for invitations, they build tables where everyone has a seat."*
>
> – T. Reneé Smith

When Women Show Up, Everything Changes

Let me take you back to 1964. A woman named Stephanie Kwolek was working in a lab, trying to develop lightweight fibers for car tires. The solution she created looked cloudy and thin—nothing like what she expected. Her colleagues told her to throw it out.

She didn't.

That "failed" experiment became Kevlar, saving countless lives through bulletproof vests. All because a woman trusted her instincts over conventional wisdom.

Or consider 1906, when Sarah Breedlove—better known as Madam C.J. Walker—was told Black women's hair care was too niche a market. She built a beauty empire anyway, becoming America's first female self-made millionaire and employing thousands of women along the way.

Katherine Johnson calculated the trajectories that put men on the moon—by hand, because she was more accurate than the computers.

Hedy Lamarr invented frequency hopping while Hollywood dismissed her as just a pretty face. That technology became the foundation for WiFi and Bluetooth.

Notice a pattern? When women enter spaces, we don't just participate—we revolutionize. We see problems others miss. We create solutions others said were impossible. We build movements that change everything.

And now? Now we're standing at the threshold of the AI revolution.

History is literally being written as you read this page. The question isn't whether AI will transform every industry, relationship, and aspect of human life. The question is: Will women be the ones shaping that transformation, or will we let others write the future while we watch from the sidelines?

Spoiler alert: We don't do sidelines.

Why This Moment Needs Us Specifically

Here's something the tech bros don't understand: AI isn't just about processing power and algorithms. It's about reimagining how humans live, work, connect, and thrive. And frankly? Women have been doing that since forever.

We're the ones who look at a problem and ask, "But how does this affect the children?" We're the ones who consider seven generations ahead, not just the next quarterly earnings. We're the ones who build businesses that feed families AND communities. We're the ones who pursue breakthrough ideas without breaking our values.

The AI revolution needs our specific genius because we think in ecosystems, not silos. We see connections others miss. We prioritize humanity alongside profitability. We ask different questions, which leads to different answers.

But here's what makes me laugh (and sometimes want to shake people): While we're worried about being "ready" for AI, AI is waiting for us to show up and lead.

The Plot Twist Nobody Sees Coming

Everyone's talking about AI replacing jobs. They're not wrong—entire industries will transform, and some roles will vanish. But you know what else is true? New opportunities will emerge that we can't even imagine yet. The difference between those who thrive and those who struggle —strategic positioning and the willingness to lead change rather than fear it.

When the internet emerged, who built the most successful online communities? Women. When social media exploded, who figured out how to build authentic connections at scale? Women. When remote work became necessity, who created systems that honored both productivity and humanity? Women.

Now AI is here, and the same pattern is emerging. While others debate and deliberate, women are quietly revolutionizing:

- Healthcare: Female doctors using AI to catch diseases earlier while maintaining the human touch that heals

- Education: Women teachers creating personalized learning that honors each child's genius

- Business: Female entrepreneurs building AI-powered companies that scale impact without sacrificing soul

- Community: Women leaders using AI to solve problems everyone said were too complex

We're not waiting for permission. We're too busy making history.

Your Invitation to History-Making

Let's get specific about what's possible when you stop watching and start leading:

The Compound Effect of Strategic Women When you master the **T.I.M.E Human-Centered AI™ Strategy Framework** and model it for others, you're not just changing your life. Every woman who watches you integrate AI strategically gets permission to do the same. She teaches five friends. They teach their daughters. Suddenly, we have a generation of women who see AI as a tool for amplification, not a threat of replacement.

The Organizational Revolution When you use the **G.U.I.D.E. Framework for Human-Centered AI™ Transformation** to lead AI transformation in your organization, you're creating a template others will follow. Your success story becomes the case study that convinces another company to put humanity at the center of technology adoption. Your approach becomes the new standard.

The Innovation Explosion Women ask different questions. When we lead AI development, we create solutions for problems others don't even see:

- AI that helps sandwich-generation caregivers manage both children and aging parents
- Technology that makes entrepreneurship accessible for women in underserved communities
- Systems that protect work-life integration instead of destroying it
- Innovations that strengthen families rather than fragment them

How to Position Yourself as a History-Maker (Not a History-Watcher)

1. **Claim Your Seat at the Table** Stop waiting to feel "ready." Stephanie Kwolek wasn't "ready" to invent Kevlar. You have the T.I.M.E. framework. You have the G.U.I.D.E. principles. You have everything you need to start leading NOW.

2. **Ask Better Questions** Instead of "How can I keep up with AI?" ask "How can AI serve my vision for a better world?" Instead of "What if AI replaces me?" ask "What becomes possible when AI amplifies me?"

3. **Document Your Journey** History needs witnesses. Share your AI transformation story. Write about your failures and breakthroughs. Your documentation becomes the roadmap for women coming behind you.

4. **Build Strategic Alliances** Find other women who understand that frameworks beat features. Create mastermind groups around the T.I.M.E. principles. Start G.U.I.D.E. implementation teams in your organization. Revolution happens in community.

5. **Think Legacy, Not Just Profit** Every AI decision you make is shaping the world your daughters and sons will inherit. Choose tools and strategies that create the future you want them to live in.

The Three Waves of Women's AI Leadership

Wave One: The Early Adopters (That's You) You're reading this book. You're learning the frameworks. You're among the first women to approach AI strategically rather than frantically. You're setting the template others will follow.

Wave Two: The Fast Followers (Coming Soon) As you succeed and share your story, other women gain courage. They see your T.I.M.E. roadmap working. They watch your G.U.I.D.E. implementation transform organizations. They think, "If she can do it, so can I."

Wave Three: The Transformation Generation (The Future) Our children grow up seeing AI as a tool for empowerment, not replacement. They enter the workforce already fluent in human-AI collaboration. They build on what we started, creating possibilities we can't even imagine yet.

Wave Four: The Forgotten Generation (We're Working to Prevent) Here's the reality we can't ignore: While we're building our movement, boardrooms filled with men are making decisions about AI that will impact every industry. Tech companies led predominantly by men are designing the future. Government policies about AI are being written in rooms where women's voices are underrepresented.

If we don't act now, there's a fourth wave—women who operate in fear, who don't upskill, who get left behind because no one showed them another way. Women whose jobs transform while they lack the skills to transform with them. Women whose voices aren't heard in crucial conversations because they weren't in the room where AI strategies were decided.

This is why our movement matters. Every woman who masters AI strategically doesn't just elevate herself—she claims a seat at tables where the future is being designed. She ensures that AI development includes perspectives on family impact, community wellbeing, and human flourishing. She helps to prevent that fourth wave by pulling other women forward with her.

What History Will Say About Us

Imagine historians in 2074 writing about this moment:

> "The AI revolution could have gone many directions. It could have become another tool of oppression, widening gaps and leaving the vulnerable behind. Instead, a movement of strategic women emerged.
>
> Armed with frameworks rather than fear, they insisted that AI serve humanity, not replace it. They built organizations where technology amplified human potential rather than diminishing it. They created systems that strengthened families while scaling businesses.

These women didn't just adapt to the AI age—they shaped it. They proved that the most powerful technology is worthless without wisdom, strategy, and soul. They showed that true innovation happens when you combine artificial intelligence with emotional intelligence, strategic frameworks with human values.

History changed because women decided to lead rather than follow, to create rather than consume, to shape the future rather than fear it."

Your Role in the Revolution

This isn't about becoming someone you're not. This is about being MORE of who you already are, with AI as your amplifier.

You're not just learning AI—you're pioneering how humans and AI collaborate beautifully. You're not just implementing tools—you're modeling strategic thinking . You're not just surviving change—you're leading transformation.

Remember: Every woman who changed history started exactly where you are—unsure but unwilling to sit on the sidelines, strategic enough to see opportunity where others saw obstacles, brave enough to begin before feeling ready.

History Makers: Your Role in AI

💭 TAKE A PAUSE, FRIEND, FUTURE HISTORY-MAKER

Before we close this chapter, sit with these questions:

1. What problem do you see that others miss—and how could AI help you solve it?

2. Whose life would change if you fully embraced your role as an AI leader?
3. What legacy do you want to leave for the women coming after you?
4. If you knew you were literally making history, what would you do differently starting tomorrow?
5. What's stopping you from starting today? (And is that reason worth missing history for?)

DO THIS NOW, NOT LATER

Action 1: Make Your History-Making Declaration Write down one specific way you'll use AI to create change others said was impossible. Share it with someone who'll hold you accountable.

Action 2: Start Your Strategic Circle Invite 3-5 women to form a TIME/GUIDE study group. Make history together instead of alone.

Action 3: Document Day One Today is literally Day One of your AI leadership journey. Document where you're starting. In one year, this becomes the "before" that inspires others.

Action 4: Choose Your Revolutionary First Step Pick one place where you'll lead AI adoption—your family, your team, your community. Start the revolution where you are.

A COACH'S NOTE ✉

My brilliant, history-making sister,

As I write these final words of this chapter, I'm thinking about you—yes, YOU—reading this. Maybe you're on a plane, in your car during school pickup, or hiding in your bathroom for five minutes of peace (I see you).

You might be thinking, "This sounds inspiring, T. Reneé, but I'm just trying to make it through Tuesday."

I get it. But here's what I know: Every woman who changed history was also just trying to make it through her Tuesday. Katherine Johnson was calculating moon trajectories while making dinner. Madam C.J. Walker was building an empire while raising her daughter. They weren't superhuman—they were super strategic.

You have something they didn't: frameworks designed specifically for navigating this revolution. You have TIME to guide your personal journey. You have GUIDE to lead others. You have a community of women walking alongside you.

Most importantly, you have a perspective this revolution desperately needs. Your questions, your concerns, your vision for how AI should serve humanity—these aren't obstacles to your leadership. They're exactly why your leadership matters.

History is being written right now. Not in some distant future, but in the decisions you make this week about how you'll engage with AI. In the conversations you have. In the examples you set. In the courage you show.

Don't wait for permission. Don't wait to feel ready. History doesn't pause for our insecurities.

The future needs your strategic mind, your human heart, and your willingness to lead even when you're still learning.

Welcome to history-making, beautiful. It looks good on you.

CHAPTER 20 QUICK REFERENCE

Key Mindset Shifts:

- Women don't just join revolutions—we lead them
- History-making starts with strategic thinking, not perfect timing
- Your questions and concerns are exactly why your leadership matters
- Frameworks beat fear every single time

Your History-Making Toolkit:

- T.I.M.E Human-Centered AI™ Strategy Framework
- G.U.I.D.E. Framework for Human-Centered AI™ Transformation
- Strategic questions that lead to revolutionary answers
- Community of women making history together

Three Waves of Leadership:

- Wave One: Early Adopters (You!)
- Wave Two: Fast Followers (Those you inspire)
- Wave Three: Transformation Generation (The future you're creating)

Your Action Step: Make your history-making declaration today

Remember: Well-behaved women rarely make history. AI-empowered women? We're about to rewrite it.

> The future won't be written by women who wait for permission. It'll be written by women who partner with AI to create change.
>
> —T. Reneé Smith

CHAPTER 21

THE MOVEMENT SHE LEADS AND SHE LOVES™

> "The strongest women don't rise alone—they create movements that lift every woman brave enough to join them."
> – T. Reneé Smith

When Women Unite, Everything Changes

When Mary Kay Ash started her cosmetics company in 1963, she didn't just create products—she built a sisterhood. Women who'd been dismissed in corporate boardrooms found themselves leading sales teams, teaching others, and building wealth together. They shared strategies at living room parties, celebrated each other's victories, and proved that when women support women in business, everyone rises. What started with nine saleswomen became a billion-dollar movement that showed women could build empires on their own terms.

In the 1970s, when mothers noticed their children struggling in traditional schools, they didn't wait for permission to create change. Kitchen tables became planning centers as women shared teaching methods, pooled resources, and launched the homeschooling movement. What started as whispered conversations between concerned mothers became a revolution that gave millions of children personalized education.

During the 2008 recession, when corporate America was laying off workers by the thousands, women saw needs that boardrooms missed. They started businesses from their living rooms—solving real problems for real people. The woman who created eco-friendly cleaning products because her child had allergies. The mother who built a virtual assistant agency because she knew other moms needed flexible work. They didn't wait for economic recovery. They created their own.

This is who we are. When faced with the impossible, we don't just survive—we create solutions, build networks, and lift each other up. We always have.

And now, as AI reshapes everything we know about work, life, and success, we stand at another pivotal moment. The question isn't whether we'll adapt, of course we will. The question is: Will we do it alone, or will we do what we've always done best and rise together?

The Psychology of Why We Need Each Other Now

There's something that happens to your nervous system when you're learning something completely new. Researchers call it "cognitive load"—that overwhelming feeling when your brain is processing too much at once. You know the feeling. It's that moment when you're staring at another AI tutorial and your brain just... stops.

But here's what those same researchers discovered: When people learn in community, something magical happens. The cognitive load doesn't just decrease—it transforms into cognitive flow. What felt impossible alone becomes achievable together.

It's not weakness. It's wisdom.

Because when Melissa shares how she used AI to analyze customer feedback and identify service gaps she'd been missing, suddenly your business blind spots have a solution. When Kim explains how she trained AI on her communication style, your email anxiety has an answer. When Jennifer shows her meal planning system, your 5 PM food panic has a path forward.

This isn't about following someone else's blueprint. It's about creating a living library of real solutions from real women facing real challenges. It's about transforming "I don't know how" into "Let me show you what worked for me."

The Hidden Cost of Going It Alone

Let's talk about something we don't discuss enough: the exhaustion of being a pioneer by yourself.

Maybe you're the only one in your organization talking about AI strategy. Maybe your friends' eyes glaze over when you talk about AI tools. Maybe your family thinks you're going through a "phase" with all this technology talk.

So, you stop sharing your victories. You swallow your questions. You pretend it's easier than it is.

But here's what isolation costs you:

- The shortcut someone else discovered last week
- The encouragement you need when self-doubt creeps in
- The celebration that makes victories sweeter

- The perspective that turns frustration into breakthrough
- The confidence that comes from seeing others succeed

You can absolutely figure out AI by yourself. You're smart and capable. But why should you have to?

What Becomes Possible When We Connect

Something extraordinary happens when women who refuse to choose between success and sanity find each other. The conversation shifts from "How do I survive this?" to "How do we thrive together?"

We Stop Apologizing In community, you realize others are using AI to pick up kids on time, automate the mundane, and create breathing room. Suddenly, using technology to support your life isn't cheating, it's strategic.

We Start Innovating When you see how another woman adapted the G.U.I.D.E. framework for her non-profit, it sparks ideas for your corporate team. Her solution becomes your inspiration. Innovation multiplies exponentially.

We Claim Our Worth There's power in hearing another woman say, "I raised my rates after implementing AI because I'm delivering more strategic value." It gives you permission to claim your own worth.

We Rewrite the Rules Together, we stop accepting that success requires suffering. We prove that you can build an empire, lead a team, AND eat dinner with your family. We model a new way forward for our kids.

The Science Behind Sisterhood

Research from Harvard Business School shows that women who participate in professional communities are 2.5x more likely to receive promotions and 3x more likely to successfully navigate career transitions. For women CEOs, the impact is even more profound—those in peer communities report 40% higher business growth and 60% lower burnout rates.

But here's what the research doesn't capture: the 9 AM text that says "you've got this," the strategy share that saves you weeks of trial and error, the "me too" that makes you feel less alone when everyone thinks you have it all figured out.

She Leads and She Loves™ isn't just community—it's your personal board of directors, your innovation lab, your safe space to be both powerful and human. Whether you're leading a team or leading a company, you deserve a place where success doesn't require a mask.

Finding Your Home in the Movement

You know that feeling when you walk into a room and immediately know "these are my people"? That exhale of recognition when someone speaks your language, shares your values, gets your struggles without explanation.

That's what we're building. Not another networking group where everyone's performing success, but a home where you can show up as you are:

- Extraordinary and sometimes befuddled by technology
- Strategic and still figuring it out
- Leading others and learning constantly
- Committed to growth and occasionally eating pancakes for dinner

This is your space to:

- Ask the "not so stupid" question (that five other women were also wondering)
- Share the messy middle (not just the polished victory)
- Celebrate the tiny win (that saved your sanity)
- Find your voice (while helping others find theirs)

The Invitation to Your Next Chapter

Right now, thousands of women are holding this book, wondering the same things you are:

- "Can I really do this?"
- "What if I'm too far behind?"
- "Where do I even start?"
- "Who will help me when I'm stuck?"

The answer to all of these questions is the same: You don't have to figure it out alone.

She Leads and She Loves™ is where your questions find answers, your struggles find solutions, and your victories find celebration. It's where the T.I.M.E. framework comes alive through real implementation stories. Where the G.U.I.D.E. principles get refined through collective wisdom. Where AI stops being scary and starts being your secret weapon.

But more than strategies and frameworks, it's where you find your people. Women who understand that leadership includes vulnerability. Who know that success includes rest. Who believe that the future belongs to those who combine technological power with human wisdom.

The She Leads and She Loves™ Movement

WOMEN TRYING TO DO IT ALL STRUGGLE IN ISOLATION

SUCCESSFUL WOMEN THRIVE IN COMMUNITY

The Ripple Effect of Your Yes

When you join this movement, you're not just changing your own life. You're part of a ripple effect that touches:

- Your kids who watch you embrace technology fearlessly
- Your husband who sees you reclaim joy in your success
- Your colleague who's inspired by your strategic approach
- Your mother who sees new possibilities for her own life
- Your community that benefits from your increased capacity
- The woman you haven't met yet who needs exactly what you'll share

Every woman who joins makes the movement stronger, wiser, more innovative. Your perspective, your questions, your breakthroughs become part of our collective wisdom.

This Is How We Change the World

Not with grand gestures or waiting for perfect conditions. We change the world the way we always have:

- One conversation at a time
- One shared strategy at a time
- One "you can do this" at a time
- One woman lifting another at a time

The AI revolution is happening whether we participate or not. But when we shape it together—infusing it with our values, our wisdom, our insistence that technology serve humanity—we don't just adapt to the future. We create it.

Your Next Move

The gap between where you are and where you want to be isn't as wide as you think. It's exactly the width of a community reaching out to pull you forward.

She Leads and She Loves™ is that community. Your community. Waiting to welcome you home.

Visit sheleadsandsheloves.com. Not tomorrow. Not after you've "figured it out." Not when you feel ready.

Today. Because the movement needs what you bring. Your questions will help someone else find answers. Your struggles will illuminate someone else's path. Your victories will give someone else permission to begin.

A COACH'S NOTE

Friend, as I write these final words, I'm not thinking about AI or frameworks or strategies. I'm thinking about you, holding this book, standing at the threshold of transformation.

You've been doing life as a high achiever for so long, carrying everyone else while wondering who's carrying you. Building success while craving significance. Leading powerfully while longing for peace.

What if I told you there's a room full of women who understand? Who've walked this path of wanting more—not more stuff or more status, but more meaning, more joy, more sustainable success?

What if you didn't have to choose between ambition and authenticity? Between technology and humanity? Between rising and resting?

You don't. Not anymore. Not when you're surrounded by women who refuse to accept those false choices.

She Leads and She Loves™ isn't just about AI. It's about proving that when women support each other in embracing change, we don't just survive disruption—we lead transformation.

Come find us. Come find yourself. Come find what's possible when brilliant women refuse to rise alone.

Your sisters are waiting.

CHAPTER 21 QUICK REFERENCE

What You're Really Joining:

- A sisterhood of women shaping the AI revolution with wisdom and values
- A living library of real solutions from real women
- Your personal board of directors for navigating change
- A movement that's rewriting the rules of success

The Research-Backed Benefits:

- 2.5x more likely to advance professionally
- 3x more likely to navigate transitions successfully
- 40% higher business growth for women CEOs in peer communities
- 60% lower burnout rates when supported by other women leaders
- Exponentially more likely to thrive while others just survive

What Makes Us Different:

- Implementation over inspiration
- Vulnerability alongside victory
- Collective wisdom over individual struggle
- Real strategies, real women, real results

Your Action Step: Visit sheleadsandsheloves.com and find your people

Remember: The strongest women don't rise alone—they create movements that lift every woman brave enough to join them.

> When women unite around change, we don't just adapt—we transform everything we touch.
>
> — T. Reneé Smith

YOUR NEXT STEPS

Your AI-Powered Future Starts Now

Beautiful sister, this isn't goodbye, it's just the beginning of our journey together. Through these pages, you've discovered how AI can transform overwhelm into ownership. You've given yourself permission to accept support without guilt and redefined success to include both achievement and peace. You've explored how AI can enhance every aspect of who you are as a woman and support you in every role you play.

But now comes the most important part: **What will you do with everything you've learned?**

The Choice Before You

You have a choice to make. You can close this book, feel inspired for a moment, and then return to the exhausting cycle of trying to do everything yourself. You can let fear of technology keep you playing small while the world transforms around you. You can continue building a life that looks perfect from the outside while feeling empty on the inside.

Or you can choose something transformational.

You can choose to see AI not as a threat to your humanity, but as a tool that amplifies it. You can choose to stop carrying burdens you were never meant to carry alone. You can choose to build a life that feels as good on the inside as it looks on the outside. A life where success includes peace, where achievement includes joy, where leadership includes love.

You can choose to lead.

The Truth About This Moment

Here's what I know about you: You didn't read this entire book because you're satisfied with mediocrity. You read it because you're a woman who sees possibilities where others see problems, who believes in growth when others choose comfort, who has the courage to embrace change when others cling to the familiar.

You are exactly the kind of woman this world needs leading the AI revolution.

Not because you understand technology better than everyone else, but because you understand that technology should serve humanity, not the other way around. Not because you're fearless, but because you're willing to act despite your fears. Not because you have all the answers, but because you're brave enough to ask better questions.

The future belongs to women who can hold both technological sophistication and human wisdom. Women who can innovate with integrity, lead with love, and create change that honors both efficiency and empathy.

That's you, beautiful. That's exactly you.

Your Next Steps (Keep It Simple)

Don't let overwhelm steal your momentum. You don't need to master everything overnight. You just need to take one powerful step:

Join the Movement

Visit sheleadsandsheloves.com and become part of the community we're building together.

This isn't about adding another commitment to your calendar—this is about finding the support that makes everything else more manageable. Inside, you'll discover which AI experiment to try first, connect with women who understand your journey, and get the guidance to implement everything you've learned in this book.

One step. One decision. One community that changes everything.

That's it. Simple. Clear. Actionable.

Because the truth is, transformation happens faster in community than in isolation. Why figure it out alone when you can rise with sisters who get it?

Your Sisters Are Waiting

Listen, I need you to hear this: The strongest women aren't the ones who carry everything alone. They're the ones who build systems, communities, and support that amplify their impact.

You don't have to figure out AI by yourself. You don't have to navigate transformation in isolation. You don't have to keep choosing between competing priorities when you could have both.

Come build this future with us. Inside She Leads and She Loves™, your ambitions are understood, your challenges are shared, and your vision for an integrated life is the norm. Here, AI isn't about replacing your humanity, it's about finally having the bandwidth to express it fully.

Until We Meet

As I finish writing these words, I'm imagining when our paths cross—perhaps at a live event, through our community platform, or when you're the one teaching others what you've discovered.

I can't wait to hear about the life you've architected with AI as your strategic partner. The hours reclaimed for what matters. The stress transformed into strategic calm. The permission you finally gave yourself to want it all—and get it.

But mostly, I hope you'll tell me that you've stopped apologizing for being multi-dimensional and started celebrating it.

The world needs your leadership. The future needs your wisdom. The next generation needs your example.

Your AI-powered future—where strategy meets soul— begins now.

> ❝ Your transformation isn't just changing your life—it's showing every woman watching that integrated success is possible. ❞

If this book spoke to the woman behind the title…

If it cracked something open—your mindset, your motherhood, your marriage, your mission— If it gave you permission to lead with humanity *and* technology...
Then this is just the beginning.

Leave a review on Amazon.com

Your words might be the exact reason another woman picks up this book and steps into her next level. Thank you for paying the transformation forward.

Ready to find your AI-powered leadership edge?
Take the **She Leads With AI™ Quiz**—
In just 3 minutes, uncover how AI can help you reclaim your time, reduce your burnout, and rise in every role you lead: **as a CEO, a leader, a change agent, a mother, a wife, and a woman.**
Start the free quiz now at www.SheLeadsWithAIQuiz.com

Craving connection with women who lead like you?
Join the She Leads and She Loves™ Community—where ambitious women learn to lead boldly, love deeply, and live whole.
We talk legacy and love. Profit and purpose. Strategy and surrender.
This is your space to be fully woman, fully leader—no masks,
no burnout, no apologies.
Join us at www.SheLeadsAndSheLoves.com

Let's Stay Connected
Follow me on social media for truth-with-love, behind-the-scenes moments, and unapologetic power. @coachtrenee

Websites
www.treneesmith.com -
Thought Leadership + AI
www.isuccessconsulting.com -
Organizational Consulting + Strategy

T. Renee Smith

www.ingramcontent.com/pod-product-compliance
Lightning Source LLC
Chambersburg PA
CBHW041746100526
44585CB00047B/2793